"What Does All This Have to Do with Me?"

"What does Abraham have to do with me? Or Isaac? Or David? Or, for that matter, what do they have to do with each other? Are their stories a miscellaneous collection of events? Or do they all fit together? And how? Didn't my world begin when I was born? Don't I live for *today*? Weren't those guys a part of something else?" Ever ask yourself these questions?

If—just *if*—you could write God a letter and be perfectly frank with Him (and you can), is it possible that it might go something like this?

> *Dear God:*
> *If You don't mind, I have a lot of questions I want to ask. Some of them might seem dumb, but I really want to know. From the very beginning I want to know* why *You did what You did, just what You were getting at. I have questions about everything that happened. But I guess my big question is: "Have You got it all together?"*
> *Signed,*
> _____

Other Regal Venture Books by Ethel Barrett

God and a Boy Named Joe
The Strangest Thing Happened . . .
Which Way to Nineveh?
The People Who Couldn't Be Stopped
The Secret Sign
I'm No Hero
Rules, Who Needs Them?
If I Had a Wish

These Regal Venture books make Bible stories come alive for readers of every age and provide exciting resources for Bible studies.

For Family Bible Storytimes
It Didn't Just Happen

GOD, HAVE YOU GOT IT ALL TOGETHER?

ETHEL BARRETT

A Regal Venture Book
A Division of G/L Publications
Glendale, California, U.S.A.

The Scripture verses used in *God, Have You Got It All Together?* are from *The Living Bible*, Paraphrased (Wheaton: Tyndale House, Publishers, 1971). Used by permission.

© Copyright 1977 by G/L Publications
All rights reserved

Published by
Regal Books Division, G/L Publications
Glendale, California 91209.
Printed in U.S.A.

Library of Congress Catalog No. 76-29 888
ISBN 0-8307-0434-5

CONTENTS

Prologue: "God, You Mean You Made a Perfect World, and Allowed Man to Mess It Up?" **6**

PART ONE
1. "You're Going to Start a Nation with *One Man?*" **12**
2. "God, Aren't You Off to a Pretty Shaky Start?" **25**
3. "*What* Great Nation?!?" **30**
4. "But God, This Nation Refuses to Grow *Up!*" **36**
5. "Will They *Ever* Get to the Promised Land?" **46**
6. "Idols, God? In the Promised Land?" **54**
7. "But God, They're Demanding a Human King. How Are You Going to Handle This?" **60**
8. "Now Your Nation Is a *Kingdom?*" **65**
9. "But God, Your Kingdom Fell Apart." **72**
10. "God, Can You Straighten Out This Mess?" **81**

PART TWO
11. "God, You Mean the Messiah You Promised Is *Jesus?*" **90**
12. "God, Isn't Anybody Listening?" **100**
13. "But God, Jesus Is Here. Doesn't Anybody Care?" **105**
14. "The Ransom Is Paid, God— Are You Going to Give Man a Choice *Again?*" **115**
15. "But God, Jesus Has Gone Back to Heaven. Is It for Good?" **124**
16. "God, You Mean You Actually Put All This in Writing?" **135**
17. "God, You Mean You Really Have It All Together? And Jesus Is Coming Again?" **148**

Epilogue: "No More Questions, God." **160**

PROLOGUE

"GOD, YOU MEAN YOU MADE A PERFECT WORLD, AND ALLOWED MAN TO MESS IT UP?"

This is a story of a great King,
And a great promise,
And a great mystery.

Once, long long ago, before the beginning of time, there was a great King. He was different from all the other kings who ever followed Him, for all the other kings had a beginning and an end.

They were born, they lived, and then they died.

Not so, this King.

He has always *been*. And He will always *be*.

He had many names,
King of kings,
Lord of lords,
Prince of Peace,
Wonderful Counselor—
And more.

Now one day (although it is quite inappropriate to call it "day," for this King does not go by days or weeks or years. He operates quite outside the realm of time.) ANYHOW, one day He flung out an incredible array of stars and planets and galaxies, vast beyond our wildest imagination. And all of this was what we know as the Universe. And He peopled this Universe with angels—or should we say He "angeled" this Universe with angels, for indeed people had not been created yet. And over all the other angels, He put one angel wiser and greater than all the rest.

And He named this angel Lucifer. And Lucifer's duty was to carry God's love and His government back to the angels.

Now there isn't time to tell the whole story here, nor do we yet understand all of the details of it—but, in a word, Lucifer became proud. And in his pride and in his conceit, he thought, "I'm not satisfied to *serve* the King. I want to be His *equal*." So he (and a vast number of angels with him) rebelled against the great King.

For this, Lucifer was thrown from the heavens—he and his angels with him.

He was stripped of his glory.

His name was changed to Satan.

And his angels were now spirits of darkness, or demons.

Now Satan in his colossal pride hadn't considered that the only power he'd ever had was the power the great King had given him. He couldn't create, for instance, for creating is making something out of nothing, and only the King could do that.

Which is exactly what the great King did next.

He fashioned the earth into a place of incredible beauty and filled it with such wonders, that on land or sea, to this very day, all of them have not been discovered.

And then He created man. He put man right in the middle of all this beauty. And He made man in His own *image*, which means He made man with a *personality*, who could think and feel and reason—and who could *love*.

For as incredible as it seems, the great King wanted man to love Him. He gave man the ability to make up his own mind, for He wanted man to love Him and do His will, because he *chose* to.

This is where Satan came back into the picture.

He couldn't create.

BUT.

If—what *if*—he could persuade man to make the wrong choice? If—what *if*—he could persuade man to choose to disobey the great King?

Which is exactly what Satan did (persuade man, that is).

The King said, "Don't do it."

And Satan said, "Do it."

And, you guessed it. Man did it. He chose to disobey the King. And by his choice, he took his life out of the King's hands.

It was as if Satan had said to the King, "I couldn't create. But I've caused man to disobey You by his own choice. And disobedience to Your will is sin. So now You've lost him. He was Your perfect creation, but he is now my slave (and believe me it will go hard for him)."

"Yes indeed I've lost him," said the King. "I've lost him but I haven't stopped loving him. I want him back. And I'll *get* him back. I'll pay the ransom and redeem him—*buy* him back. And I will free him from the slavery of sin."

The Great Promise

And this is where the PROMISE came in.

For right then and there, the great King made a covenant with man. Now a covenant is a promise. The one who makes the promise is the covenant*or*. And the one who receives the promise you might call the covenant*ee*.

From here on out, we'll call the promise THE COVENANT.

Anyhow, right then and there, the King made a promise that in due time He would pay the ransom and redeem man, buy him back for His very own.

For as you've guessed by now, the great King was God. The first man was Adam.

God was the covenant*or*.

Adam was the covenant*ee*.

But it goes beyond that. For God was not just looking at Adam. He was looking down through the ages. . . .

The Great Mystery

And the mystery? Actually it's a mystery loaded with clues. They are all about us, in everything God made and did and said. As you read this book, you'll find out what they are.

But let's get back to the story.

? • • •

The human race multiplied upon the earth. And sin multiplied too.

By the time many hundreds of years had gone by, God had had enough.

The Bible tells us that on all the earth there was only *one man* who was obeying God.[1] *One man!*

His name was Noah, and you know his story well.

He is the one who preached to the people. And built the Ark. And was saved from destruction when the roaring flood destroyed mankind.[2]

Noah and his family obeyed God.

• • •

Then God brought up the subject of the COVENANT again. And He told Noah that it would be EVERLASTING.[3]

After the flood, a new civilization was started. And, you guessed it, man blew it again.

Meanwhile Satan remained very busy. He still had power on earth, but only as much as God allowed him to have. He could not be everywhere at once. He was wholly dependent on a vast host of demons, some of them in high places, some of them underlings, but all subject to him.

• • •

And God?

He had not abandoned His plan.

He was going to zero in on a *nation* now. And call out for Himself a special people.

"No matter," said Satan. "I messed it up before and I can mess it up again. If we work hard enough at it, things can go uncomfortably from bad to worse."

• • •

And thereby hangs a tale of seemingly incredible adventure and derring-do.

1. Genesis 6:6,8.
2. God destroyed mankind, but not without warning the people first.
3. Genesis 9:16,17

BUT IT'S ALL TRUE!
Read on!!!

• • •

Checklist
Does God have it all together? Check it out and see: (The list will grow as you read on.)
 1. God made a covenant with man.
 2. Man blew it.

PART ONE

CHAPTER 1

"YOU'RE GOING TO START A NATION WITH *ONE MAN*?"

"You interrupted Me when you stopped at Haran. And settled down. I didn't tell you to settle down."

It was God speaking. And then,

"Canaan," God went on, "I wanted you to go to the place I'd show you. Remember?"

What was *this* all about?!?

Well, you'll see in a minute, but right now we have to go back a bit.

• • •

God had a plan for the redemption of man.

There was only one catch.

He chose to use MAN to carry it out.

And from the garden of Eden to Noah, man had blown it at every turn.

But God wasn't finished yet.

He had just begun.

What did He do next?

Well, out of the entire world, He called a special people, and set them apart for His very own. A nation, set apart, belonging to God!

Now He had to start somewhere. And He started with ONE MAN.

A man who lived in UR, in southern Mesopotamia.

• • •

The city of Ur sprawled in the desert, its temples and libraries and houses gleaming white in the sun. It was a beautiful city, cooled by

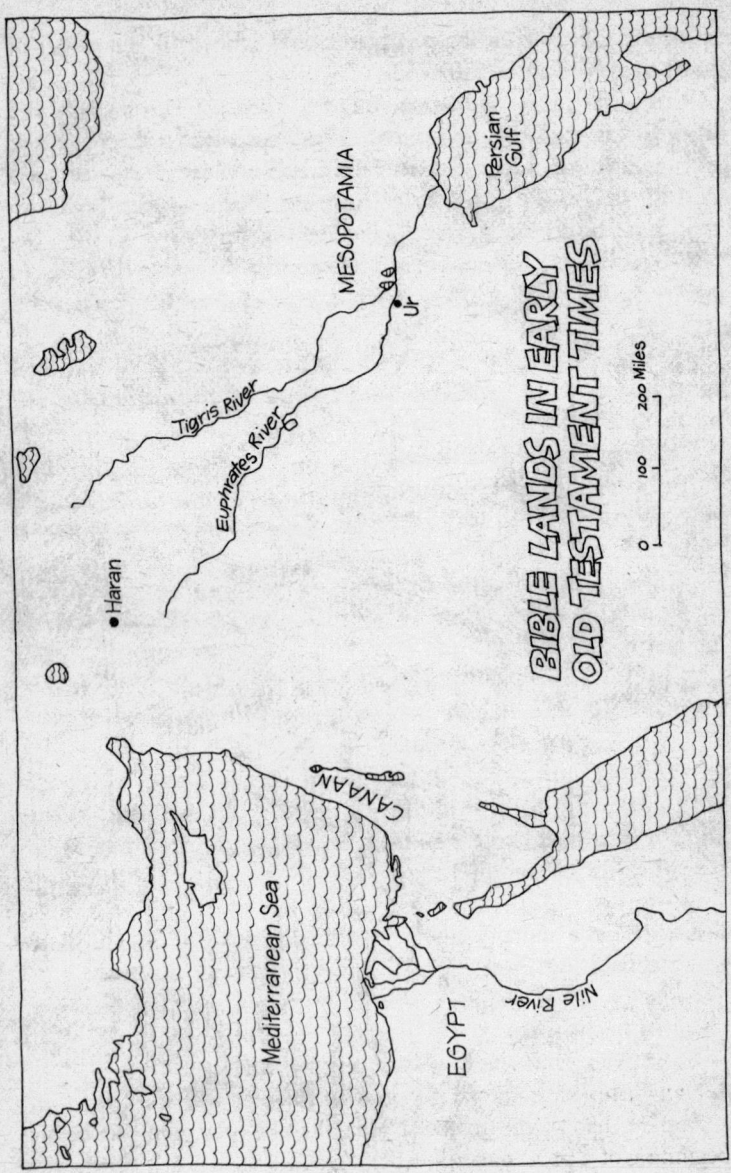

splashing fountains in the courtyards, and fanned by the clatter of palm trees blowing in the wind.

And it was a busy and prosperous city. From the Persian Gulf and from Egypt, the treasures poured in—alabaster and copper ore and ivory and gold and hard woods. They came over the great waterways of the Nile and the Tigris Rivers, and the Mediterranean Sea. And they came by caravans through Canaan and Egypt.

The people of Ur lived in comfortable two story houses of brick and plaster, built around courtyards, with plenty of room for families and servants.

Students struggled with their reading and writing and math and square root, for the education and culture of that civilization was highly developed.

Children laughed at their play,

And babies squawled and gurgled,

Or screamed in terror as they were killed and sacrificed to Nana.

Nana wasn't a kindly grandmother.

Nana was the moon god—an idol.

For with all its beauty and all its wealth, the city of Ur was without any knowledge of God.

What?!?

God called a man out of *this* city to start a nation of His own.

The man's name was Abram.

Whenever we think of Abram, we think of some kind of a saint who was called out of the wilderness, his feet barely touching the ground, and the light streaming down from heaven on his head, and violins playing in the background.

Not so.

Abram was a man of wealth and influence, rich in flocks and herds, and gold and silver too.

He had a father Terah,

And a nephew Lot,

And a wife Sarai who was very very beautiful.

He worshiped the moon god and he studied the stars.

And he hadn't the remotest idea that he was going to be the beginning of a great nation.

God spoke to *Abram?*

Why Abram had never even been on speaking terms with God!

But deep in Abram's heart, something was stirring, and the Holy Spirit of God was at work. For with God, nothing happens by accident. When He calls a man to do a job as important as starting a nation, He knows perfectly well what He's doing.

"God, Just What Are You Up To?"

Just exactly HOW God called Abram that first time, we are not really sure. We are sure, however, that God did speak to Abram somehow—and that Abram listened.

The Bible tells us (in Acts 7:2,3) that "God appeared to our ancestor Abraham in Mesopotamia,

And told him to leave his native land,

And to start out for a country *that God would direct him to.*"

And that is exactly what Abram did.

When he told his wife Sarai, she probably thought, "*A tent? Me live in a tent? Me leave this comfortable house and all my friends and live in a tent?*"

But there is no record that she dragged her feet.

She went along willingly.

It is even more remarkable that Abram's old father Terah was willing to drop his idol-worshiping, and go along too.

Abram's nephew Lot was game for adventure; he packed up his family and went along happily—no questions asked.

And so they started out.

Where to?

They just started following the trade route north. It was like hearing someone drop one shoe, and waiting for him to drop the other one.

They had their cattle, and all the possessions they could carry on camels and donkeys.

And home was wherever they could pitch a tent.

Off they went, leaving all the comforts of life behind, traveling up alongside the Euphrates River, over 600 long weary miles—to Haran.

And there they stopped

"God, Isn't Abram a Bit of a Risk?"

Haran was in the middle of a network of trade routes. It was easy to collect more possessions there, and Abram did.

But though they had traveled all those miles, they were STILL in Mesopotamia.

Ur was in the *southern* part of Mesopotamia.

And Haran was in the *northern* part.

Whether they chickened out, we don't know. At any rate, they decided to stay awhile.

Perhaps it was because of old Terah.

Poor old Terah. Though his spirit had been willing, his body was weak, and it was there in Haran that old Terah died.

"God, Are You Still Counting on This Man?"

Then God spoke to Abram again.

"Abram," God said, "I'd like to pick up this conversation where we left off, before we were so rudely interrupted."

"Interrupted, Lord?"

"Yes. You interrupted Me when you stopped at Haran. And settled down. I didn't tell you to settle down."

"Go on, Lord."

"Canaan," said God. "I wanted you to go to Canaan. Remember?"

"Yes Lord," said Abram.

"Leave your own country behind," said God. "Make a clean break. And go to the land that I will guide you to. And if you do, I'll cause you to become the father of a great nation.[1]

"I'll bless you,

"And make your name famous,

"And you'll be a blessing to many others. The WHOLE WORLD will be blessed because of you."[2]

Why this was no daydream. Clearly God was up to something very definite, and He meant business.

---

1. This great nation would first be called the "Hebrew" nation, and God's people would be called "Hebrews."
2. Genesis 12:1-3.

This was a *covenant*.
With two sides![3]
God promised to bless Abram and make him the father of a great nation. *But Abram had to obey*.

This was an earth-shaking, life-changing COVENANT.
Phew!
This time Abram did as the Lord had instructed him.
He took his wife Sarai,
And his nephew Lot,
And all his wealth. He had a lot of cattle and servants by this time.

They trekked across the desert, sandblasted and weary. And finally got to the land of Canaan.

Then God "dropped the other shoe." "I'm going to give this land to your descendants," He said. This was *it!*

And Abram built an altar there to celebrate God's visit.

• • •

It was at this point that Satan began to get uneasy. Apparently things were not, as he had hoped, going to go "uncomfortably from bad to worse." He sent a communique to his warlords:

Greetings from the pit:
　A rather disturbing thing has happened. As you know, I'd hoped that everything was well in hand, and that God had quite given up the human race.
　But now I find that instead of giving *up* the human race, He is planning to call *out* of the human race—a great nation for His very own!
　And He has called ABRAM from the city of Ur, to start it!
　He has already told Abram to go to the land of Canaan. And what's more, Abram has obeyed. He left his home town of Ur, went up the Euphrates River to northern Mesopotamia. I thought for awhile that he was going to get side-tracked in the city of Haran and stay there. But to my dismay, he moved on. And guess where he is now?

3. Sort of like a contract!

In Canaan. Right where God told him to go. What's more, he has built an altar to God. And what's *more*, he's trekking all over the land God promised him and is building altars to God wherever he stops.

Now, as Abram cut his teeth on idol worship, I am not too disturbed at the moment. I don't think he's going to hack it. Perhaps if things got uncomfortable enough in Canaan he could be persuaded to leave.

If you have any ideas on the matter, let me know. Meanwhile I think the fellow will bear watching. Perhaps, with any luck, he'll make a major mistake.

I have decided to take no chances; I am declaring a state of alert.

                      Your master in the desolate den
                      Satan

"How to Be the Father of a Great Nation Without Really Trying."

Well, the two things Satan had hoped for, happened.

First, Abram was made uncomfortable. There was a great famine in the land of Canaan. And second, he not only made one mistake; he made *two*—and they were big ones.

He panicked during the famine, packed up his family, and took them all off to EGYPT.

That was his first mistake.

And as they neared the borders of Egypt, he made the second one.

"Sarai," he said, "You're very beautiful. If the Egyptians know you are my wife, they might kill *me*, so they can have *you*.

"BUT,

"If you say that you are my SISTER—"

Ah yes. If they thought she was his sister, they not only would spare his life, but they would treat him royally.

Cagey, that.

Cagey—but still a lie. Actually it was only a half a lie. Sarai was Abram's *half* sister. But a half a lie is as bad as a whole one, any day it will do quite as well.

Abram's hunch was right. When they got to Egypt, everyone spoke of Sarai's beauty, until the news reached the Pharaoh. And the Pharaoh promptly took her into his household. And showered Abram with gifts—sheep, oxen, donkeys, camels—and slaves to boot.

Now of course the Lord wasn't going to stand still for this. So he promptly sent a plague[4] on Pharaoh's household.

It didn't take Pharaoh long to figure out what had happened. Not the disease, but the reason for it.

He sent for Abram.

"What have you done to me?" he bellowed. "Why didn't you tell me this woman was your wife? Why were you going to let me marry her, thinking she was your sister?"

Abram just stood there, his hands dangling, his tongue cleaving to the roof of his mouth.

"Take her!" screamed Pharaoh, "And be gone!"

And he packed them off in fury, and sent them all out of the country with an armed guard.

Abram was richer, all right.

He had twice as much silver and gold and cattle and slaves as he'd had before.

But he was sadder.

And wiser too.

He had two mistakes against his record.

● ● ●

And as if that weren't enough, Sarai made a big mistake too.

Time after time, God had told Abram that He would make of him a great nation. And time after time, Abram would answer, "But Lord, how can this be when I have no son?"

And each time God would answer, "You *will* have a son. Just wait."

God told him and told him.

"Look up into the heavens," God would say, "and count the stars if you can. Your descendants will be like that—too many to count." And, "Look as far as you can," God would say, "in every direction. I'm going to give it all to you and your descendants. And the nation that will come from your family will be like the dust—too many to count."

4. **Horrible disease.**

Yes, God told him.

Abram told Sarai, too.

But in spite of all this, Sarai made *her* big mistake.

"Abram," she complained, "ten years have gone by and still we have no son. *Ten years.*"

And she took her maid, whose name was Hagar—an *Egyptian* girl—and gave her to Abram to be his second wife.[5]

Such a business!

Well, in time, Abram and Hagar had a son. They named him Ishmael.[6]

But it wasn't the way God had planned it.

It was the way *Sarai* had planned it.

• • •

Satan was delighted. "Abram has a son," he chortled. "But he is NOT the child of promise. Things couldn't be more mixed up. I couldn't have planned it better myself."

"God, Are You *Still* Going to Give Abram That Son?"

But Satan's spirits did not stay high for long.

For God renewed that covenant[7] with Abram, and in no uncertain terms. No doubt about it, God meant business.

"I'll guarantee to make you into a mighty nation," He said, "And what's more, I'm changing your name. You are no longer Abram.[8] I'm going to call you ABRAHAM. This means 'Father of nations.' *For that's exactly what I'm going to make you.*"

WELL INDEED!

"This is not a short-term covenant," God went on. "It's forever. And incidentally I'm changing your wife's name too. It is no longer Sarai. I'm going to call her SARAH. And this means 'Princess.' And I will give her—yes, *I will give her a son.*"

---

5. This was a no-no! God had a special plan for Abram's family.
6. It was through Ishmael that the Arab nation has come. These people have been bitter enemies of the Jews down through the ages and even up to this very day.
7. Contract, remember?
8. Exalted father.

Wow.
Satan was horrified.
This was definitely a turn for the worse.
And Abraham?
Well, Abraham was laughing inside. He couldn't help it. He was a hundred years old!
And Sarah was ninety!
"Me—and Sarah—to have a baby?" he thought. It was too much. After twenty-five years of waiting, he just couldn't believe it.
When he told Sarah, she couldn't believe it either.

• • •

It was not long after that, when they both got quite a jolt.
It happened this way.
Abraham was sitting outside his tent in the heat of the day. He stared at a lazy fly buzzing nearby. Then he got sleepy. Then he started to doze. *Then* he sat up straight.

There were three strangers coming toward him, in the distance. He roused himself, and with all the courtesy of a man in his position, hurried out to meet them. "I pray you," he said, "stop and rest awhile and be my guests. I'll have water brought so you can wash. Here, sit down."

And then, "Sarah!" he called. "Sarah, we have guests. Quickly! Some of your best cakes. And some meat! Oh, and some cheese!" he called back over his shoulder as he hurried off to give some orders.

He had a fatted calf killed and fixed.

And Sarah bustled about with the servants, getting the flour and preparing the delicious cakes. There was milk and butter and the fresh roasted meat. And cheese. And all the trimmings.[9]

It was the thing to do in those days. When you dropped by a wealthy man's tent, you got the royal treatment, even if you were a stranger.

The men sat there eating and drinking and talking. It was like any typical visit in the Orient.

But suddenly the conversation took an unexpected turn.

9. This menu wasn't "Kosher," but "Kosher" hadn't been invented yet.

"Where is Sarah, your wife?" they asked.

"In the tent," he said with some surprise.

And then, the bombshell.

"Next year," one of them said, "I will give you and Sarah a son."

What was this? Next year *I* will give you and Sarah a son? *I*?!?

Why—why—one of those men was the Lord Himself![10] Abraham was stunned.

So was Sarah.

For she was inside the tent, listening.

She might have been stunned, but she still couldn't help laughing inside. "*Me* have a baby?" she laughed. "Me, ninety years old? And with a husband who is a hundred?"

Then the One who was the Lord said to Abraham, "Why did Sarah laugh? Why is she thinking to herself, 'Can an old woman like me have a baby?'"

Suddenly it was no laughing matter.

"Is anything too hard for God?" The Lord said quietly.

There was a great silence.

Then He went on. "Next year Sarah will have a son— *just as I told you*."

Sarah was shaking. "I didn't laugh," she said at the tent door. It was a lie and she knew it.

And she knew they knew it too.

She had lied because she was afraid.

But a lie is a lie, for any reason, and she lowered her eyes in shame and was silent.

Then the men left.

Abraham walked on with them a way. After awhile he came back, his feet scarcely touching the ground. For a long time, he and Sarah sat, and in hushed tones, repeated the scene over and over again.

The presence of God!

And at long last, after twenty-five years, the promise of a son!

---

10. Though Abraham had never heard of Him by that name—it was Jesus! Jesus was with God from the beginning of creation, though He did not come to the world as a baby until thousands of years later (John 1:1,18).

Unbelievable.
But somehow, suddenly they had to believe it.

● ● ●

Satan had to believe it too. Things were going badly, badly indeed.
Well, he would wait it out, he decided. It bore watching all right. In spite of Abraham's blundering, God might still have His way.

● ● ●

Abraham and Sarah did have that son. One year and one blunder[11] later, the baby was born.
God had kept His promise. He had begun to fulfill HIS side of the covenant.[12] For that son was the child of promise.
Well, they named him Isaac.
And Isaac meant "laughter."
And the years were filled with laughter indeed.
Laughter and joy.
Abraham and Sarah's troubles were over at last. The years that followed were serene and trouble-free.
Five years,
Ten years,
Twelve years. Twelve wonderful years.
And then it seemed as if the sky fell in.

Checklist

"God, do You have it all together?" Check it out and see:
 1. God made a covenant with man.
 2. Man blew it.
 3. God called out a special NATION for Himself, and chose Abraham to be the father of it and gave this nation THE PROMISED LAND.
 4. God made a covenant with Abraham, gave him a son (Isaac) and promised to bless Abraham—*if he would obey*.

11. Abraham had a fracas with King Abimelech; you can read about it in Genesis, chapter 20.
12. The Promise, remember? Like a contract!

CHAPTER 2

"GOD, AREN'T YOU OFF TO A PRETTY SHAKY START?"

"The Sky Is Falling!"
"Abraham!"
"Yes, Lord?"
"Go to the land of Moriah."
"Yes Lord."
"Go to one of the mountains there that I'll point out to you."
"Right, Lord."
"Take Isaac with you—"
"Yes Lord."
"—Isaac whom you love so much—"
"Right, Lord."
"Take him with you—and sacrifice him there as a burnt offering!"
What?!!!!?
Yes indeed, the sky had fallen in.
Abraham lay in the dark, his heart numb with despair.
When dawn came, he was still awake. He hadn't slept all night. He got up, chopped the wood for a fire on the altar, and saddled a donkey. By that time the others were awake. The wood and provisions were loaded on the donkey, and with Isaac and two servants, Abraham started out for Moriah.
It was a three day journey; Abraham had plenty of time to think.

Why would God give him a child of promise only to take him away again? And, if he killed Isaac on the altar, would God—COULD God—bring him back to life? Is anything too hard for God, he kept telling himself, is *anything* too hard for Him?

By the third day of the journey they were all too tired to talk. They approached Mt. Moriah in silence. Then, "Stay here with the donkey," Abraham told the servants. "Isaac and I will go up to the Mount alone, to worship. Wait for us."

And he hiked the wood for the burnt offering up on Isaac's shoulders.

"Do you have everything?" Isaac asked him.

"Everything," said Abraham.

"The knife and the flint for the fire?"

"Yes."

The two of them went on together. And then,

"The lamb for the sacrifice?" Isaac said at last. "Father, where is the lamb for the sacrifice?" There was a long silence as they trudged on.

"God will take care of it, son," Abraham said.

At the top of the mountain, they built the altar and laid the wood. And then Abraham turned to Isaac, and began to tie him. "I have to do it," he said softly, and his voice trembled.

Now Isaac was a big strapping boy of twelve and full of ginger. He could have fought; he could have run in panic. But he did none of these things, for the Bible tells us that he lay on the altar, and Abraham took his knife—

And he lifted it up—

And he got ready to plunge it into Isaac's breast—

And at that moment—"Abraham—Abraham!"

It wasn't a whisper; the voice of God shouted it from heaven.

"Yes Lord," he answered.

"Lay down the knife."

Abraham did, trembling.

"Don't harm the lad. I know that I am first in your life. You have not withheld even your son from Me. Now turn around."

Abraham did. And there behind him was a ram caught by its horns in a bush. God had provided the sacrifice! Abraham took the knife, the tears trickling down his beard and bouncing off. And he killed the ram.

The thing was finished, the test was over. And he'd passed it!

"But God, Do You Think This Is Going to Hold Up?"

Later, God brought up that covenant[1] again. "Because you have obeyed Me," He said, "I will bless you and multiply your descendants into billions of people, like the stars in the sky and the sands on the seashore."[2]

Abraham sighed a deep sigh and looked sideways at Isaac trudging along beside him. All the billions of people, this new nation God was calling out—hung on one person, this twelve-year-old boy. And he was still alive.

• • •

"Yesssssss," hissed Satan. And he scribbled a memo:
My dear Fiends:

As you know, the latest developments are gloomy. Not critical, but gloomy.

For awhile I was quite content with Abraham's blundering. His wife Sarah played right into our hands too. But now things have taken a glum turn.

Their son Isaac—(and God's new nation depends on *that one son*)—that miserable lad was within one whack of a knife from death—and God spared him the last minute. I'm furious to have to report that Isaac is alive and well, and from the way it looks, he's going to do everything right and escape from our clutches.

Be not discouraged however; I've just begun to fight.

Your master,
Prince of Darkness.

P.S.: The state of alert is still in effect.

• • •

Isaac was indeed still alive and he stayed alive for a long, long time.

1. Contract. Remember?
2. See Genesis 22:16-18.

And from there on out, Abraham did everything right. Isaac, his child of promise, was absolutely the only one who could carry on God's plan for a great nation, a special people, for Himself. He must be guarded and brought up well.

He was.

We don't have any record that he as much as stubbed his toe.

He must marry the right girl and have lots of children.

He did.

Abraham sent a servant all the way back to his own country, to the city of Haran, to find a girl from his own people for Isaac to marry. Her name was Rebekah and she was willing to be Isaac's wife.

And so Isaac married Rebekah.

And Abraham's job was done.

"God, Does Our Believing You Make Up for Our Blundering?"[3]

With all of his blundering, one thing can be said of him. *Abraham believed God.* And God paid him the highest honor in all the world any person could ever hope for. He said it in four words.[4] It was simply this—

He was My friend. . . .

Checklist

Does God have it all together? Check it out and see:

1. God made a covenant with man.
2. Man blew it.
3. God called out a special NATION for Himself, and chose Abraham to be the father of it and gave this nation THE PROMISED LAND.
4. God made a covenant with Abraham, gave him a son (Isaac) and promised to bless Abraham if he would obey.
5. God tested Abraham's obedience; Abraham passed the test.

---

3. Yes!
4. See Isaiah 41:8.

CHAPTER 3

"WHAT GREAT NATION?!?"

The great nation God had promised was on its way. Abraham was dead, but Isaac and Rebekah were left to carry on. They were married and settled there in the Promised Land.

And that's when Jacob came into the picture.

Jacob and his brother Esau were twin boys who were born to Isaac and Rebekah.

And what a sorry twosome they were!

Some people in life are "givers." And some people are "grabbers." Jacob was, unfortunately, a grabber. He snarled at his brother Esau from the day they were born.[1] His motto in life was "I want what I want when I want it." If it didn't belong to him, he schemed and connived to get it. And as he grew older, the one thing he wanted more than anything else in his life was the birthright when his father Isaac died.

Now the birthright was very important. The son who got the birthright, got twice as much of the inheritance as the other children. He was the head of the household and therefore the boss. And he was the head of the household spiritually too.

It was all right for Jacob to wish he had the birthright. But there was one little problem. The *elder* brother was the one who was supposed to get it. And Esau was the elder brother. It was all right for Jacob to *want* it. The way he went about *getting* it was quite another matter.

He knew one of Esau's greatest weaknesses. Some people eat to live; Esau lived to eat. His god was his belly, and all he could think of was what his next meal was going to be. Jacob knew that Esau's downfall could be something as simple as a good stew. It was at least worth a try.

So he waited until Esau went on a long hunting trip, and he cooked

1. Esau snarled back at him too.

up a delicious stew with herbs and spices. And the odor of it was so delicious that when Esau came home he could smell it fifty yards away.

"I'm starving to death," he said. "It smells delicious. Give me some."

This was the moment Jacob had been waiting for. "I'll swap you some for your birthright," he said.

"I'm dying from hunger!" Esau moaned, "What good is my birthright going to do me? *Please* give me some."

"And the birthright?" Jacob insisted.

"All right, all *right*," said Esau. "Take it, it's yours."

"Swear that you'll give it to me first."

"All *RIGHT*!!"

In a few minutes the stew was gone. And so was Esau's birthright. All Jacob had to do now was wait it out, until Isaac was old.

"God, Are You Going to Hang All Your Plans on *This* Family?"

When the time came, Isaac was not only old, he was nearly blind. It was easy for Jacob to pretend that he was Esau and go in and kneel before his father and get the blessing and the birthright.[2]

And what's more, Rebekah[3] helped him. She not only helped him carry out his scheme to get the birthright, but she helped him run away after it was all over, so Esau wouldn't kill him. She told old Isaac that it was time Jacob went back to the home of her family in Haran to find himself a wife. And she packed him some provisions and sent him on his way quickly before Esau could get at him.

It was a bit of a mess all around.

• • •

Satan rubbed his hands together and hummed in F minor. "This little drama is shaping up much to my liking," he thought. "Rebekah is a schemer, Jacob is a grabber, and Esau can think of nothing beyond his own belly. What a family. This should be easy. They're all

---

2. How he did it is a very interesting story. You can read about it in Genesis 27.
3. Isaac's wife and Jacob's mother, remember?

losers." And he sat down to write a memo to tell his warlords to buck up, they weren't finished yet.

But neither was God.

"But God—Jacob Is a Schemer!"

Jacob sank down to the ground, exhausted. It was sundown and he had been walking since dawn. He took a large stone and put it under his head for a pillow, and fell asleep almost at once.

Suddenly—

A vivid dream!

The most vivid dream Jacob had ever had in his life.

There was a ladder, reaching clear up to heaven, and the angels of God were going up and down on it. Jacob looked up, up, up to the very top—

And there stood the Lord Himself! "I am the God of Abraham," He said, "and of your father Isaac." And He repeated the same covenant[4] promise to Jacob as he had given to Abraham. "What's more," He said, "I'll protect you wherever you go, and I'll be with you until I have finished giving you all that I have promised."

Then the ladder, God, and the voice were all gone.[5]

Jacob sat up in a cold sweat. He was terrified. "God lives here!" he thought. He lay back down on his stone pillow, trembling.

He was still thinking about it the next morning when he got up. He took the stone he'd been using for a pillow, and set it up on end for a monument. "If God is going to be with me like that," he vowed, "and protect me—then He shall be my God. This stone will be a memorial to Him."

He packed up his provisions and turned to go. He gave one last backward look. "And all that You give me, Lord," he said, "I'll give a tenth back to You."

"Good grief," Satan moaned, "this is incredible. The Lord isn't finished with this man yet."

No, the Lord was far from finished with Jacob. There were a lot of edges to be evened off him—he was far from smooth.

4. That contract again.
5. Though Jacob had never heard of Him by that name—it was Jesus!

"Good for You, God—Jacob Met His Match!"

Jacob went back to Haran. It was there he married his cousin Rachel. And it was there he finally met his match.

His match was Uncle Laban.[6]

Now, if Jacob was a schemer, his Uncle Laban was a bigger one. If Jacob was a cheater, Uncle Laban was a worse one. If Jacob was a swindler, Uncle Laban was the inventor of swindles.

For years, the two of them grabbed and cheated and swindled. They swindled each other out of land and cattle. They spent twenty-one years trying to out-swindle each other—

Until Jacob finally took his wives and children and cattle and went back to live in the country with his old, old father Isaac. But first, he had to make peace with his brother Esau.

"What's in a Name, God?"

It was on his way back to meet Esau that his greatest encounter with God happened. Suddenly, in the dead of the night—a man appeared mysteriously out of the shadows. And began to wrestle with him!

On and on they wrestled, until the first streaks of light appeared off in the east. "Let me go," the man said, "for it is dawn."

But Jacob hung on for all he was worth. "I will not let you go," he cried, "until you bless me!"

And then came the biggest turning point in Jacob's life.

"Your name is no longer Jacob," the man said. "Your name is now ISRAEL—which means A PRINCE WITH GOD." And the man blessed him. And then he was gone.

It was then that Jacob realized that he had been wrestling with—the Lord Himself!

Jacob did not know Him by name, but it was Jesus!

And all the deceit, and all the craftiness, and all the grabbiness in Jacob's nature seemed to roll away. He, at long last, had become what God wanted him to be.

He got up, and went on his way—*limping*[7]—toward home, to make up with his brother Esau.

---

6. His mother Rebekah's brother.
7. And he limped for the rest of his life!

"Everything's in Bits and Pieces."

Now if Jacob had spent the first half of his life being a grabber, he spent the last half of his life paying for it.

His beloved wife Rachel died. As far as he knew, his favorite son Joseph was killed by wild beasts.[8]

And now, finally, in his old age, there was a famine in the land. The only hope for survival was for Jacob to send his sons into Egypt where they might be able to buy some corn. Things looked bleak; things looked bleak indeed.

• • •

"Things look bleak for them," Satan wrote to his warlords. "Where's this great nation we've been hearing so much about? *What* great nation? Why, they've gone through three generations—Abraham, Isaac and Jacob—and they're still just a struggling family—can't even get along with each other." He signed it with a flourish—"from your master in the desolate pit."

Indeed, it did look as if God had abandoned the whole idea. Everything was in bits and pieces.

Checklist

Does God have it all together? Check it out and see:

1. God made a covenant with man.
2. Man blew it.
3. God called out a special NATION for Himself, and chose Abraham to be the father of it and gave this nation THE PROMISED LAND.
4. God made a covenant with Abraham, gave him a son (Isaac) and promised to bless him if he would obey.
5. God tested Abraham's obedience; Abraham passed the test.
6. God appeared to Isaac's son Jacob and renewed the covenant promise again.

---

8. Or so he thought. Actually Joseph's brothers had sold him. You can read the story in Genesis 37.

CHAPTER 4

"BUT GOD, THIS NATION REFUSES TO GROW *UP*!"

"God, Is This the Happy Ending?"

Everything in bits and pieces?

Not on your life.

God had His eye on every bit and every piece, and when He got around to it, they were going to fall into place.

One of the "pieces" was that Jacob's beloved son Joseph had not died after all. His brothers had sold him as a slave and he had been taken into Egypt. There, after a thrilling story of ups and downs,[1] he had come into great favor with the Pharaoh. And had been given a position of power and influence. In fact he was the governor of the land!

Then, when the famine came to the Promised Land where Jacob lived, he sent his other sons to buy corn to—of all places—

Egypt!

The rest of the "pieces" fit together with uncanny precision. [2]

Joseph recognized his brothers—

Sent them back home loaded with grain—

Invited his father and his brothers to come to Egypt to live—

Which is *exactly* where God wanted them at that particular time—

Ha!

"You Mean Jacob Made It?"

And so Jacob and his family packed up their duds and loaded their camels and donkeys and carts and made the happy trek to Egypt. With all their cousins and in-laws there were seventy of them, not

---

1. You can read Joseph's long and exciting story in Genesis 37-50.
2. Right on the nose!

counting their women and children and slaves. And there was as dramatic and thrilling a reunion as you could ever hope to see.

Jacob's name was indeed ISRAEL at last.

The whole set-up in Egypt was custom-made for them. They lived in the land of Goshen near the Nile River, right in the midst of the most advanced civilization of that day. They had a chance to get the best of education, instruction and training in all the arts and in all the industries of that culture, as if somebody had planned it all. And indeed somebody had. God Himself had planned it.

You might say they lived happily ever after, and it would be true. For Jacob (Israel) spent the rest of his life there in happiness. And died there.

And so did all of his twelve strong sons and their families.

But before we leave Jacob—

With all his faults and all his weaknesses, always remember that he wound up being called ISRAEL. And his descendants were called ISRAELITES.[3] They could have been called Abrahamites.

Or Isaacites.

Or Josephites.

Or even Mosesites.

But they were forever after called Israelites.

At long last, God's nation was getting off to a start.

There in beautiful trouble-free Goshen, the descendants of Jacob stayed. And there they grew.

And grew.

And *grew*. And several hundred years went by.

"God, You've Got Satan Worried!"

Several hundred years later, Satan dashed off another memo (time means nothing to Satan; he does not live in time).

Dear Muckrakes:

Something is going on here in Egypt that will bear watching. These Israelites have grown and grown and grown until they are bursting the seams of the land of Goshen. These twelve strapping

3. Remember, God's people were first called "Hebrews"? Well now they were called "Hebrews" and also "Israelites"!

sons of Jacob, who got his name changed to Israel—these twelve strapping sons have grown into twelve great tribes. And all told, they number approximately *two million* people, give or take a few. Now by anybody's calculation, that's a lot of people and that's a nation to reckon with.

I've been watching them through my network of demons for several hundred years, and I've become discouraged as the centuries rolled on. For no matter how I scheme, they seem to be able to do nothing but prosper.

I keep hoping an ill wind will come along and blow them off the map. We can only wait and see.

Meanwhile, let's keep in touch; report to me any news you might be able to pick up.

Your patiently waiting (and hating) master,
Satan

"God, Couldn't You Have Let 'Well Enough' Alone?"

Satan didn't have long to wait. The period of physical training had ended.

Now it was time for the spiritual training to begin.

And it began with trouble. For, without warning, all those years of peace and prosperity came to a grinding halt.

A Pharaoh had come into power who didn't know who Joseph was and didn't care. All he cared about was the population explosion that was going on in the land of Goshen. And he was alarmed. So he made slaves of the Israelites and put the most brutal taskmasters over them. They worked from sunup to sundown on the most backbreaking burdens—toiling in the fields and building the cities Pithon and Raamses. But the worse he treated them the more they grew. So he finally commanded—

—that all newborn boys—

—*be thrown into the Nile River*!

There was one baby boy, however, who didn't make it to the river to drown. He made it to the river in a little boat his mother had fashioned from papyrus leaves. And there he was hidden among the reeds along the river's edge, when one of Pharaoh's daughters came along with her maidens to bathe.

She spied the boat—
Took the baby—
and adopted him!
And the baby you know well. She named him Moses.

"God, Are You Going to Hang All Your Hopes on *This* Man? He Looks like a Loser."

Moses was brought up in the palace, and given the advantages of all the wealth and culture and education of Egypt. And then, in one split second, he threw it all away and ran for his life.

He had come upon an Egyptian taskmaster brutally beating an Israelite slave.

And he had killed him.

And buried him in the sand.

And before you could say Princess Hatshepsot[4] Moses had fled the country and was halfway to Midian.

There he married and settled down and went into the sheep business with his father-in-law. That would have been the end of it—except for one thing.

"God, Why Didn't You Choose Somebody *Bolder*?"

One day he was tending sheep on the back side of a mountain,[5] when he saw a bush aflame. But the bush was not being *burnt*. He walked toward it in amazement.

Then he heard the voice. *"Don't come any closer. And take off your shoes. You're standing on holy ground."*

Moses knelt, and covered his face with his hands.

"Yes, I am the God of your fathers," the voice went on, *"the God of Abraham and Isaac and Jacob."*

---

4. Archeologists believe that Hatshepsot was the princess who adopted Moses. Her son-in-law hated her so much that after she was dead he had the noses broken off all of her statues. The statues are there to this day—with all their noses gone! This has nothing to do with the story, but it's interesting. Well, isn't it?
5. Exodus 3.

After all these years—the God of Abraham, Isaac and Jacob!!!

"*I have heard the cries of my people and am come to deliver them out of Egypt—BACK TO THE PROMISED LAND.*"

"Yes Lord," whispered Moses.

"*I am going to send a leader to Pharaoh to demand that he let them go.*"

"Yes Lord," said Moses, a little louder.

"*That leader is YOU.*"

"No Lord," whispered Moses.

If ever a man tried to get out of doing a job, it was Moses that day. But God finally convinced him he was the man for the job.

Then came a reunion with his brother Aaron whom he had not seen in forty years.

And together, the two of them went to Pharaoh to demand that Pharaoh let the Israelites go—

Out of slavery—

Out of Egypt—

And BACK TO THE PROMISED LAND.

Well!

"God, You Mean Their *Safety* Hinged on a Sacrificial Lamb?"

There followed a succession of miracles, such as there had not been in hundreds of years. Abraham had never seen the like of it. Isaac had never seen the like of it. Jacob had never seen the like of it. There was an absolute EXPLOSION of God's power.

You know the story well. Several astonishing miracles and ten plagues later, the Israelite nation (for now it was the beginning of a great nation)—poured out of Egypt toward the Promised Land.

It was so big that it's hard to imagine. It was like two million people bursting out of Chicago and heading for the midwest plains.

Wow!

But, the night before they left, something happened that was to become one of the greatest and most significant events in all of God's plan. The very people who went through it did not fully realize its importance at the time. It was not until thousands of years later that it became clear just what God was getting at.

You will read about that later on in this book.

But here's what happened that night.

After nine plagues had not persuaded Pharaoh to let the Israelites go, the tenth disaster was announced in advance. The eldest son would die—in every family—from the lowliest, right up to the *Pharaoh's*!

Incredibly, after all that had happened, Pharaoh would not listen. He was going to have to learn the hard way.

Meanwhile, the Israelites got their instructions:[6]

Every family had to get a lamb—a perfect lamb, without blemish. And kill it. And sprinkle the blood on the doorposts of their homes.

And that night they were to eat roast lamb,

And bitter herbs,

And bread *without yeast*.[7]

They were to eat with their traveling clothes on, prepared for a long journey,

Wearing walking shoes and carrying walking sticks, ready to GET GOING when the signal was given.

Sure enough,

That very night, the angel of death went through the land and took the oldest son in every family. EXCEPT in the homes where the blood was on the doorposts. "When I see the blood," God had said, "I will *pass over you* and you will not be punished."

Not one Israelite home was touched.

Their safety had all hinged on the lamb.

The lamb that was killed, and the blood that was sprinkled on the door.

"You must celebrate this Passover feast every year," God said, "For it will cause you always to remember when I brought you out of the land of Egypt. And tell your children, so *they'll* remember."

They vowed they'd never forget.

"They're Safe at Last—Or *Are* They?"

And then this incredible mass of people poured out of Egypt,

6. Exodus 12.
7. No time for yeast; the bread would take too long to rise!

loaded down with jewels and gold and silver the Egyptians had given them, and headed for the Promised Land.

It was while they were camped by the Red Sea that Pharaoh decided to chase them.

"God, Your Plan Is Done For!"

Satan was delighted. He scrawled a hasty memo to his warlords:

Dear Slubberdegullions:

I take my pen in hand to write you a message of triumph!

But first, the bad news. God led those Israelites (He led them by a pillar of cloud by day and a pillar of fire by night) first toward the wilderness, then right up to the Red Sea.

But now the good news! Pharaoh is after them with six hundred chariots and a huge army! And would you believe it, they are trapped between the sea and the desert. I feel sure they are done for—and so do they. You should hear them wail! It looks as if God's plans are all awash—or all dried up, depending on which way those wretches decide to flee!   In any case, I'll keep you posted.

                Your master,
                Prince of the Bottomless Pit

"God—This Is Brain-Straining!"

But God's plan was far from "done for." He told Moses to stretch his staff over the waters—and the most eye-boggling thing happened!

First, the Sea *parted*!

Then a wind blew all night,

And dried the bottom,

And the whole mass of them walked through the Red Sea on dry ground!

Now this is brain-straining. A little boy came home from Sunday School once, and told his mother about it. "When they got to the edge of the Red Sea," he said, "they brought out their pontoon bridges, and they got out their amphibious tanks—" And he went on to describe some of the most brilliant military strategy that you ever heard. "Come *on*," said his mother, "You *know* it didn't happen that way." "I know it didn't, but if I told you how it really did happen, you wouldn't believe it."

It *was* hard to believe. Everything had been hard to believe right from the beginning. Way back in Midian when God had said, "The Pharaoh will let you go and I'll see to it that you'll be loaded down with goods when you leave—silver and gold and jewels and the finest of clothes." And Moses had said, "They won't believe me. They'll never believe You appeared to me."

Satan could hardly believe it either. He was absolutely seething with rage when he wrote his next memo:

My Muckrakes:

You're not going to believe this; I can hardly believe it myself. I tremble as I write.

I told you the Israelites were stranded between the desert and the Red Sea. Well not for long, my evil ones, not for long. God told Moses to order them to march. 'March?' I thought, 'March *where*?' Well, as it turned out, they marched clear across the Red Sea on dry land—after God parted the waters!

But that, my dear muckworms, was not the worst of it. The Egyptian army *followed* them. But God caused the Egyptians' chariot wheels to come off. And before they could scramble out of there, the waters closed again.

The Israelites are safe on the other side. Pharaoh's army is drowned. And I am seething with rage!

However, let us not be discouraged in evil doing (I keep telling myself). They have the wilderness ahead of them. And anything can happen. Let us hope for the worst.

Your old master,
Satan

• • •

Yes, anything could happen—
and did.
Bitter water, no water at all, hunger, attacks from enemies.
And worse.
Much worse.

Checklist

Does God have it all together? Check it out and see:

1. God made a covenant with man.
2. Man blew it.
3. God called out a special NATION for Himself, and chose Abraham to be the father of it, and gave this nation THE PROMISED LAND.
4. God made a covenant with Abraham, gave him a son (Isaac) and promised to bless him if he would obey.
5. God tested Abraham's obedience; Abraham passed the test.
6. God appeared to Isaac's son Jacob and renewed the covenant promise again.
7. God led His nation to Egypt and left them there for 400 years so they could grow in numbers, then raised up Moses to lead them back again to THE PROMISED LAND.

CHAPTER 5

"WILL THEY *EVER* GET TO THE PROMISED LAND?"

"But God, Anything Could Happen!"

Yes, anything could happen—and did.

But each time the Hebrews ran into trouble, God delivered them. When they found the water at Marah bitter, God showed them how to sweeten it.

When they were hungry, God rained down manna from heaven.

When they were thirsty, God told Moses to strike a rock. And water gushed out.

He gave them victory when they were attacked by enemies.

He prevented their clothing and shoes from wearing out.

He led them by a pillar of cloud by day and a pillar of fire by night. All this—and more![1]

But Satan was not discouraged. "Never fear," he said to his warlords, "I have given them a grumbling spirit. And a grumbling spirit always leads to trouble."

Unfortunately, he was right.

"Why must we die of thirst?" they grumbled.

("See how ungrateful they are," said Satan.)

"Oh that we were back in Egypt!"

("See how they moan.")

"Give us water!"

("See how they wail.")

"Is God going to take care of us or not?"

("See how they doubt.")

And then they got to Mount Sinai.

---

1. Too much to write in this book. You can read it all in Exodus 15-18.

Moses climbed the rugged mountain to get his instructions from God. And left his brother Aaron in charge.

And God made a covenant[2] with Moses, just as He had made one with Abraham and Isaac and Jacob.

That covenant again!

"I brought you to Myself," God said, "as though on eagle's wings. Now. If you will obey Me and keep *your* part of the covenant, you shall be My own nation out of all the nations on the earth."

If you will obey Me—

There were those same terms again!

He would make them a great nation—

AND THEIR PART WAS TO OBEY.

Moses went back down and told the people all this.

"We will certainly do everything He asks of us!" they shouted.

("See how they put their foot in their mouth," hissed Satan.)

Then, in the midst of smoke and thunder and lightning, God gave them the Ten Commandments.

Plus a host of other laws.

"We will obey them all!" they cried.

("There goes that foot again," said Satan.)

Then Moses climbed the mountain again. The Ten Commandments were written on tablets of stone. And God gave him instructions to build the Tabernacle.[3]

And the Ark of the Covenant.[4]

This time Moses stayed up in the mountain forty days and forty nights.

("I'll keep you posted," Satan wrote to his underlings. "They are without Moses for awhile. We'll see what they do now.")

---

2. No escape from that contract. The Promise goes on.
3. It was a tent for worship.
4. The Ark was a chest about 45-inches long, 27-inches wide and 27-inches high, made of acacia wood and covered with pure gold. On each side were two golden rings with poles inserted for carrying it. The lid was made of solid gold and on it were two angels of gold, with outspread wings. And what was inside? Why, the stone tablets with the Ten Commandments on them. A golden pot of manna. And Aaron's rod that God had caused to bud. It was to remind the Israelites of God's presence.

It was even worse than Satan had hoped. When Moses came down from the mountain—they were worshiping a golden calf!!

Moses exploded to his brother Aaron. And demanded an explanation.

"Well, they thought you'd disappeared, and you weren't coming back," said Aaron. "So they asked me to make them a god to lead them."

"And?"

"Well, I asked them to give me their golden jewelry. And I threw the jewelry into the fire—"

"*And?*"

"Well—up came this calf," Aaron finished weakly.

Satan was walking back and forth with glee. It did look as if everything was finished.

Moses smashed the tablets of stone to the ground.

And God decided to abandon the whole idea![5]

He really threatened to, and indeed He would have done so, but Moses, of all people, pleaded with Him to forgive this baby nation doing everything wrong—and give them another chance.

The Ten Commandments were written *again*.

And a weary, disobedient people again stumbled on their way.

Somehow, during the wandering, they managed to get the Tabernacle built.

And the Ark of the Covenant.[6]

A camp was organized—

Every tribe had its place—

And God still hovered over them with love and mercy.

It was an eleven day march to Kadesh-Barnea—the very edge of the Promised Land.

Satan's warlords were getting nervous.

"Don't worry about it," Satan comforted them. "Just keep injecting into them the spirit of grumbling and the spirit of doubt. And let's hope that before they get into the Promised Land, they'll blow it."

5. Call the whole thing off.
6. Exodus 25-27.

Now you'd think that when they got right to the edge of the Promised Land, they'd shape up and smile. But, sure enough—

"Oh No, God—Not *Again!*"

They blew it. Yes, *again*.

Moses sent twelve spies into the Promised Land to look it over. And though they came back with fruit that had grown so huge they had to carry a cluster of grapes on a pole between two men—their report was straight from the spirit of doubt.

"The people are like giants!" they bellowed.

"The cities are surrounded by thick walls!" they gloomed.

"We're like grasshoppers, compared to them. They'd *pulverize* us!" they moaned.

Well, between the spirit of grumbling and the spirit of doubt—they managed to come through the test with one big zero. The grumbling and doubting spread through the whole camp like one big howl.

"We won't go into this new land!"

"We'd rather die here in the wilderness!"

They had said it and said it and said it, in the past.

But this time they'd said it once too often.

"God, Aren't You Being a Little Rough on Those People?"

"All right," said God, "You *will* die here in this wilderness. You will wander in this wilderness for FORTY YEARS until every last one of you lies dead in the desert. Your children will go to the Promised Land. But not a single one of you will ever see it."

In all of this hubbub, two of the spies had held out. They kept insisting that it was all right to go over into the land, that God would be with them. But, with all the wailing and all the moaning, nobody heard them.[7]

So God gave the Israelites what they wanted. They had to go back and wander in the wilderness for forty years.

Now forty years is a long time. The adults got old and died. And

---

7. The two spies were Joshua and Caleb. You'll hear more about them later, especially Joshua.

their children grew up. And *they* wandered around in circles, moving from place to place seeking pasture for their animals. Until after forty years they were right back at Kadesh-Barnea again—right back where they were before.

Right on the edge of the Promised Land.

And Satan kept them grumbling and doubting every step of the way.

"We're making progress," he kept assuring his warlords. "But I'm a little concerned about Moses. That fellow is holding up well. He's holding up *too* well. He's been holding up for forty years. For forty years they've been grumbling and he's been putting up with it.

"We might try injecting a little of the spirit of impatience in him. Try it, and see how we make out."

Unfortunately, they made out very well.

"—And Even *Rougher* on Moses?"

It happened right on the edge of the Promised Land.

This time they had no water.

Now God had given them water before. And they should have believed Him this time. But the spirit of doubt had grown strong within them.

"Take your rod,"[8] God commanded Moses. "Call the people. And *speak* to the rock."

Moses stood by the rock and looked down at the people.

"Why did you make us leave Egypt?" they wailed.

Oh no. They're not going to bring that up again!!!

"You brought us here to get rid of us!"

Moses sighed with weariness. They sounded just like their parents.

"Why there isn't even enough water to drink!"

Moses came apart at the seams.

"Listen, you rebels," he shouted. "Must *we* bring you water from this rock?"

We?

What's with this "*we*"?!?

8. This was the rod that God had given Moses at the beginning, the one he had used at the Red Sea.

Instead of speaking to the rock, he lifted his rod and—
WHAM!
He struck it with all his might.
And, WHAM!
Struck it again.
And water came gushing out.
God had told Moses to SPEAK to the rock.
And Moses had STRUCK it.
So God called him up to the top of Mount Pisgah to SEE the Promised Land.
But He told him he couldn't go over and ENTER it.
That was THAT.
Moses didn't say "Lord—whoever can take my place?"
The spirit of impatience had left him entirely.
He was God's man again.
"Lord," he said, "Appoint a new leader for the people, one who will lead them into battle."
No quibbling. He left the choice to God.
And God said, "Go get Joshua."[9]
And Moses? Still no quibbling. He charged Joshua to be faithful. And he said good-bye to his people. And on top of a mountain[10] he had his last talk with God on earth. And there he died. And there God buried him. No one has ever known the exact place.

"God, Doesn't Satan Ever Give Up?"

Satan took out his pen and dipped it in venom[11] and scratched happily away.

Dear Runnagates:

Moses is gone. God would not allow him to go over into the Promised Land. Joshua has been appointed their leader.

Now, the thing to do, I think, is to inject the spirit of *fear* into Joshua. I don't think we can get him with pride, but with fear we may have a better chance.

9. Joshua was one of the two spies on page 50. Remember?
10. Mount Nebo.
11. The poison snakes and spiders secrete.

At any rate, we'll back off for the present. But I caution you to observe him closely and we'll see what kind of a man he will be. One step at a time, I always say, one step at a time.

The Old Serpent

Checklist

Does God have it all together? Check it out and see:

1. God made a covenant with man.

2. Man blew it.

3. God called out a special NATION for Himself, and chose Abraham to be the father of it, and gave this nation THE PROMISED LAND.

4. God made a covenant with Abraham, gave him a son (Isaac) and promised to bless him if he would obey.

5. God tested Abraham's obedience; Abraham passed the test.

6. God appeared to Isaac's son Jacob and renewed the covenant promise again.

7. God led His NATION (Israel) to Egypt and left them there for 400 years so they could grow in numbers, then raised up Moses to lead them back again to THE PROMISED LAND.

8. God's nation (Israel) got to the very edge of the PROMISED LAND, and blew it again; they had to go back and wander in the wilderness for forty years.

CHAPTER 6

"IDOLS, GOD? IN THE PROMISED LAND?"

"God, Are You Trusting *Joshua* to Lead Them into the Promised Land?"

Joshua!!! *Who*?!!???

The chap who ran Moses' errands, and followed Moses around like a shadow?

The very same.

The chap who followed Moses up to the mountaintops and stayed at a distance while Moses went ahead to talk with God?

That's the one.

Joshua.

He'd never in all his life been anything but a second banana.

Now he was suddenly the leader of that wailing, grumbling, groaning mob—the Israelites. And he had no Moses to back him up.

But he had God.

And one of the first things that God talked with him about was his *fear*.

"You're the new leader," God said. "I will not fail to help you." (But then he added, "Be strong and brave.")

"You'll be a successful leader, Joshua," God said. (But then He added, "Be strong and courageous.")

"Obey the laws Moses gave you and see that the people do," God said. (But then He added, "Be bold and strong.")

"I am with you, Joshua, wherever you go," God said. (Then He added, "Banish fear and doubt.")

Well, clearly, if Joshua had to be told not to be afraid four times in one conversation, Satan must have been successful in injecting into Joshua's mind a wee bit of the spirit of fear.

BUT.

The *important* thing God had said was, "You must obey the laws Moses gave you, Joshua, and see that the people do too."

Ah, there it was again. The covenant![1]

God promised to bless them. IF THEY OBEYED HIM.

After this big talk with God[2] Joshua passed God's instructions on to the people.

"We will obey you just as we obeyed Moses!" they cried. "May God be with you as He was with Moses. Lead on!"

Oh no. It was beginning to sound like a broken record.

But Joshua had received his marching orders and he had to take the people at their word. So he issued his first command.

They were to cross the Jordan River.

"You Mean They Got Over at Last?"

On the other side of the river was the city of Jericho. Joshua sent two spies on ahead, to see where it was best to cross the river, and to spy out the city.

Satan and his warlords were waiting with bated breath,[3] hoping for the worst. They had two things in their favor. First: It was flood season and the Jordan was a raging monster overflowing its banks. Second: The spies had hidden inside the city in the home of an innkeeper named Rahab, but the news that they were in town had already reached the king and there were soldiers out looking for them.

"Things could just swing our way," said Satan.

They *could*, but they *didn't*.

1. Or contract or Promise. Got it?
2. Joshua 1:1-9. There are no LITTLE talks with God.
3. They were holding their breath in suspense.

The soldiers found Rahab's house all right. But she told them the spies had been there—and gone. It was a lie, and they swallowed it.

So the spies got back to Joshua and told him everything was GO. And Joshua and a million Israelites crossed the Jordan[4] and got safely to the other side, carrying the Ark of God with them. [5]

There they landed. There they rested. And there they celebrated the Feast of the Passover to remind them of that last fearful night in Egypt. There was no more pillar of cloud, no pillar of fire, no more manna. Now the ARK OF GOD was in their midst, and God's presence was shown *by that Ark*.

The long weary trek through the wilderness was over.

A new day was dawning.

for at long, long last—

THE PROMISED LAND!

WOW!

● ● ●

But Satan wasn't thinking "Wow." He was thinking "Aaaaaaaugh." He dashed off a quickie memo to his warlords:

Dear Riffraff:

What do you *mean*, you can't "get at" Joshua? *Watching* him isn't going to do any good. *Devour* him, *break* him. Where's your spirit? While you dabble, he has led the entire nation across the Jordan River and into the Promised Land. And with the Ark of God! I ought to rip you apart. This is the worst disaster we've suffered since Moses crossed the Red Sea!

You say he clings so closely to the Lord you can't touch him? Bah and humbug! There is *always* a loophole—get up off your haunches and find it!

Meanwhile, right under your very noses, they've celebrated the Passover!

Fie on you! Hooligans!

Your Satanic Majesty

---

4. Read this thrilling story in I'M NO HERO.
5. The Ark of God was that chest made of wood and covered with gold. It was to remind the Israelites of God's presence, remember?

"And Their Troubles Are Over?"

The days went by. And the months went by, and the years. And Joshua and the Israelites in the Promised Land had their ups and downs. But during this period, they were mostly "ups."

Joshua's rule goes down in the Bible as one long list of victories. If there had been newspaper headlines they might have gone something like this:

JOSHUA VICTORIOUS OVER 31 KINGS!

ISRAELITES CONTROL LAND OF CANAAN!

COUNTRY AT REST FROM WAR

JOSHUA CELEBRATES 100TH BIRTHDAY

Right.
Time for Joshua to wind up his affairs. Which he did.

"But God, Can't You Allow a *Few* Idols?"

He called the people together at Shechem.

He reminded them of the promises God had made through Abraham,
Through Isaac,
And Jacob,
And Joseph,
And Moses—
Right down to that very day. And that *God had kept every promise He had made.*

"Yeaaaaah!!" they said.

"BUT," said Joshua, "if you turn away, and worship other gods—He will wipe you out!"

"Ooooooooooh," they said.

"*For there are still idols in this land,*" he reminded them. "*So choose you this day whom you will serve!*"

And they shouted back, "WE CHOOSE THE LORD!"

"Then," cried Joshua, "Destroy the idols!"

"Yeaaaaaaah!" they shouted back. "We will. We will worship and obey the Lord alone!"

"God, Satan Got His Foot in the Door."

"This doesn't look too good," Satan's warlords said. "This chap has really done his homework. He's run a tight ship, he has. There's very little in Canaan right now that's bad. *Just a few idols sprinkled here and there.*"

"*Aha!*" Satan snapped back. "That's all we need. That's quite enough to get our foot in the door. Here an idol, there an idol—it's not much to go on, I'll admit. But we'll make the most of it."

And was Satan right. Was he *ever* right.

For things turned out worse than he had even hoped.

Checklist

Does God have it all together? Check it out and see:

1. God made a covenant with man.

2. Man blew it.

3. God called out a special NATION for Himself, and chose Abraham to be the father of it, and gave this nation THE PROMISED LAND.

4. God made a covenant with Abraham, gave him a son (Isaac) and promised to bless him if he would obey.

5. God tested Abraham's obedience; Abraham passed the test.

6. God appeared to Isaac's son Jacob and renewed the covenant promise again.

7. God led His NATION (Israel) to Egypt and left them there for 400 years so they could grow in numbers, then raised up Moses to lead them back again to THE PROMISED LAND.

8. God's nation (Israel) got to the very edge of the PROMISED LAND, and blew it again; they had to go back and wander in the wilderness for forty years.

9. Joshua finally led the Israelites over to the PROMISED LAND. They conquered it—*except for a few idols sprinkled here and there.*

CHAPTER 7

"BUT GOD, THEY'RE DEMANDING A HUMAN KING. HOW ARE YOU GOING TO HANDLE THIS?"

"But God, Would a Few Idols Do Any Harm?"

Was Satan right. Was he *ever* right! Here an idol, there an idol—that's all it took.

Joshua had tried to warn them. "If you're going to obey God and you really mean it," he'd said, "*get rid of the idols.*"

"We'll get rid of them" is what they *said*.

But leave them around is what they *did*.

The Israelite armies had swept through the Promised Land all right. But instead of sweeping through and driving the Canaanites out as God had commanded—they'd swept through and settled down alongside them.

And that's when things began to come apart at the seams. First they got chummy with the Canaanites. Then they began to get chummier. And *chummier*. Then they began to marry them. Then—you guessed it—they began to worship their pagan idols.

God kept raising up leaders.[1] But if they'd been rated on a scale of "Good, Better, Best"—some of them would have rated GOOD. Some BETTER. But none BEST.[2]

"Isn't It Okay to Do Your Own Thing?"

And the Bible tells us that *everyone did what he wanted to—whatever seemed right in his own eyes.*[3]

Satan's communication with his warlords took a different turn, now.

1. They were called Judges.
2. Except Samuel. More about him later.
3. See Judges 17:6.

My dear Scamps:

Keeping in touch is getting more difficult than it used to be. These Israelites have spread out all over the Promised Land. As you know, I cannot be every place at once, so I will have to have faithful reports from you from every quarter of the land to keep me informed as to what is going on.

I understand from your reports that since Joshua's death, the Israelites have gone uncomfortably from bad to worse. This is terrific! I am never so happy as when the Israelites are miserable, and I'm never so miserable as when they are happy.

Now as I see the picture, from your reports, leaders keep rising up, and they have a few years of victory—but as soon as the leaders die, the Israelites go off into a slump again.

These "leaders" (what a sorry lot!) haven't given us too much trouble. Except for a few of them.

That Gideon, for instance. I instructed you to put into his mind the spirit of fear and inferiority.[4] And a fine job *you* did. You had him nearly paralyzed with fear—you could have finished him off—and you let him slip through your fingers. Don't tell me you didn't. I know better. For after God spoke to him and gave him the go-ahead sign, he wound up with the courage of a tiger.

You did a better job on Samson—but not quite enough. True, you made him take the talent and ability God had given him and throw it all away in self-indulgence.[5] But at the end of his life, why oh why did you let him repent? He repented, and his faith in God enabled him to pull down the temple of Dagon into a heap of rubble around his enemies. Now I'm afraid he's going to go down in Israelite history as one of the heroes of faith.

I'm very pleased, however, with the job you've done on the Israelites in general. You've sold them on the idea that to "do your own thing" is the way to go. And they've certainly "done their own thing" with gusto. Every one to his own way and every one to his own pleasure—the sky's the limit.

---

4. I'm not as smart or important as other people.
5. I want what I want when I want it.

And have they paid for it, oh have they ever paid.

They are more than just divided.

They are *scrambled*.

Since God first called out this nation to be His own, I cannot remember when they've been so mixed up. Why their enemies[6] have even captured their holy Ark of God! It's gone from their presence and most of them don't even have the sense to care! And that holy Ark of God is the most valuable possession they've ever had.

Well, all in all, I'd say you did a very good job.

Your Master, the old serpent,
Satan

P.S. There is one man, however, who worries me. It's that last judge, Samuel. He has been faithful to God since God called him when he was a small boy. Nothing seems to shake him up. But you must not be discouraged. There must be *some* flaw in him. You'll find it if you watch him closely. He's way overdue to make a mistake.

And please don't come back at me with the weak excuse that he just doesn't make mistakes. It's up to you to see that he *does*.

And *quickly*.

If all else fails, put it into the minds of the Israelites to kick the fellow out.

"God, What Are You Going to Do Now?"

Well, Satan's warlords had several ways to go. They could wait for Samuel to slip. Which would be tough. For Samuel was no ordinary judge. He was a great prophet, and a great spiritual leader, second only to Moses.

The plan that worked the best—and they'd learned this clever strategy from their master Satan—was to scatter abroad in the land, and put into the minds of the people the old "We want one because everybody else has one" spirit.

And it worked.

The Israelites began to complain again.

---

6. The Philistines. Read 1 Samuel 4-6.

"Kinnnnnnnnng!" they cried. "We want a king! Everybody else has one!"

"Lord, did you hear what those people said?" cried Samuel.

"I heard."

"But they're tossing me out!" Samuel persisted. "They're throwing me out like a gunnysack full of old boots!"

"They've been tossing ME out for years," said God.

"But what shall I tell them?" said Samuel.

"Give them their king."

"*Give them their king?*"

"Yes," said God. "They're going to have to learn the hard way."

Checklist

Does God have it all together? Check it out and see:

1. God made a covenant with man.

2. Man blew it.

3. God called out a special NATION for Himself, and chose Abraham to be the father of it, and gave this nation THE PROMISED LAND.

4. God made a covenant with Abraham, gave him a son (Isaac) and promised to bless him if he would obey.

5. God tested Abraham's obedience; Abraham passed the test.

6. God appeared to Isaac's son Jacob and renewed the covenant promise again.

7. God led His NATION (Israel) to Egypt and left them there for 400 years so they could grow in numbers, then raised up Moses to lead them back again to THE PROMISED LAND.

8. God's nation (Israel) got to the very edge of the PROMISED LAND, and blew it again; they had to go back and wander in the wilderness for forty years.

9. Joshua finally led the Israelites over to the PROMISED LAND. They conquered it—*except for a few idols sprinkled here and there.*

10. The "few idols" turned into "many idols" and everyone in the nation "did his own thing." They finally demanded a king.

CHAPTER 8

"NOW YOUR NATION IS A KINGDOM!"

"That Covenant Again?"

"Kinnnnnng! We want a king! Everybody else has one!" the Israelites cried.

"They're tossing me out!" Samuel told God.

"They've been tossing *Me* out for years," said God. "Give them their king. They're going to have to learn the hard way."

So Samuel set about to find the king of God's choosing.

His name was Saul.[1]

And that's when the subject of the covenant[2] came up again.

"Here's your king," Samuel told them. "And if both you and your king follow the Lord your God, all will be well with you. BUT. If you continue to sin—you and your king will be destroyed!"[3]

There it was again. Two sides of that covenant!

"God, Satan Is Making Short Work of *This* One."

"Pssssssst," said Satan to his warlords. "That man Saul could be dangerous to our cause. The people adore him. And he seems to be a nice humble chap. (I hate people like that.) Put into his mind the spirit of jealousy. And a strong desire to have his own way. We just might trip him up on one of those nasty little sins."

And trip him up they did. Saul's desire to have his own way was so strong that he rode roughshod[4] over God's orders. And he wouldn't listen to Samuel's advice.

1. Israel entered a new era (a whole new ballgame). This was the beginning of a long line of kings.
2. Right, contract!
3. 1 Samuel 12.
4. Like a bulldozer.

And when DAVID[5] came on the scene—!

Saul was so jealous of David's popularity that he went from scowling at him—

To throwing javelins at him—

To chasing him all over the country to kill him.

Now no king is going to stay in the seat of honor for long with those kinds of shenanigans.

And Saul didn't.

He began to run down like a wooden clock.

And he finally died in disgrace.

And David was declared the new king of Israel.

"God, Is Satan Winning?"

"I'm not worried," said Satan. "Why nearly a thousand years have gone by since God made that first covenant[6] with Abraham. And since then, not one thing—*not one thing* has gone right for them. In the covenant, God promised to make them a great nation. But *their* side of the covenant was to obey,

"To stay out of sin,

"To stay away from idols.

"And they've never kept their promise.

"Not once.

"If they weren't falling down on one point they were falling down on another. And sometimes, when we really worked hard on them, they were falling down on all of them at once.

"They don't have a chance. Why don't they give up? Why?—"

"Isn't This Something New?"

But wait a minute. What was this?

This covenant God made with David *was not like any covenant He'd ever made before*.

Not like the one with Abraham.

Or Isaac.

Or Jacob.

---

5. That's David the shepherd boy, the one who killed Goliath, remember?
6. Or Promise.

Or Moses—
None of them.
What was *this*? "Your family shall rule My kingdom *forever*"?[7]

And this? "I have taken an oath to establish David's descendants as kings *forever* on his throne—from now until eternity?!!???"[8]

Run that by again?
Forever? No matter *what*?

That could mean only one thing. That promise God had made to Adam *way* WAY back in the garden of Eden at the beginning of the world, He firmly intended to keep.

That was why He'd spoken to Abraham and called a nation out for Himself.

That was why He'd guided this nation through Isaac and Jacob and Joseph and Moses and Joshua and all the Judges and Samuel and Saul and David—

Phew!
And now this!

"God, Is *This* What You Were Getting At?"

Now He had narrowed it down to a *family*. He was calling out a family—a family to be established by David, that would go on and on and ON until—

the Messiah would be born! God would come to earth as a man, born as a baby. From this special family!

A Saviour.
JESUS!

"Satan Got Your Point, God."

"This is the worst news since the Universe began," said Satan.

"Can't you find something wrong with it?" his warlords wanted to know.

"No!" he screamed. "It's absolutely unconditional. After this, when they disobey, they'll be punished. *But the contract will still be binding.*

7. Read 2 Samuel 7:16.
8. Read Psalm 89:4,28,30-34.

God's promises are sure. They stand fast. There's nothing we can do to shake them. But—"

"What?" they wanted to know.

"The only thing we can do is make them *hinder* God. Make Him put it off."

They thought about that for awhile.

"It's the only thing I can think of at the moment," Satan said finally. "Delay, delay, delay. One step at a time. Meanwhile, we can only hope for the worst."

● ● ●

Now if there was any man Satan wanted to knock out of the race—it was David. But David's actions seemed to defy him at every turn.

"Keep him from finding a center of government," Satan ordered.

And David captured Jerusalem and made it the capital.

"Keep him from having a center of worship!" Satan cried.

And David brought back the holy Ark of God[9] and put it in the center of Jerusalem.

"Keep him from being organized!" Satan tried again.

And David proceeded to organize the country—did he ever organize it! It had never been so thoroughly united.

"Then keep his kingdom from growing!" Satan was frantic.

And David expanded his kingdom in every direction.

"Destroy him!" Satan shrieked.

"We can't," they said. "We've been trying to destroy him for years. No way."

"All right, then," Satan said, "Attack his *personal* life. I'd rather attack him in a way that would foul up the whole nation, but it doesn't seem possible. So we shall have to be content with fouling him up personally. See to it. See that he sins."

"God, Satan Has His Foot in the Door!"

They did.

And, unfortunately, David did.

9. It had been captured by the Philistines, remember?

He took his general Uriah's wife for his own. And he sent Uriah into battle to be killed.

Satan was delighted. "We've got him, we've got him, we've got him at last!" he chortled.

But David was crushed over what he'd done. He confessed his sin to God.

And he repented with great sorrow.

And he asked God to forgive him.

And God did.

"Why did he have to go and repent?" screamed Satan. "Saul didn't repent. I kept Saul under my thumb till the very end. And we almost had David, we almost had him! I hate him for asking for forgiveness. He's undone all my hard work."

"All is lost," his warlords said.

"Perhaps not," said Satan, brightening a bit. "Sin bears fruit. He will have to pay for what he has done. Perhaps *all* is not lost."

• • •

David did have to pay for his sin. For one thing, he longed to build a magnificent Temple for the Lord in Jerusalem. The days of the tent-Tabernacle were over. And David dreamed of a permanent Temple where people from all over the country could come to worship.

But God said no.

He gave David the *plans* for the Temple in great detail. But he told David that his son Solomon would be the one to build it.

David had other personal trouble too.

His son Absalom rebelled against him. And tragedy followed his children and his family all during his life.

• • •

"His troubles are like gnats, buzzing about his head," gloated Satan. "And he cannot brush them away."

Indeed they did "buzz about his head" to the end of his life.

But he died in honor, loved by his people.

"We worried him, though, to the very end of his life," Satan's warlords comforted him.

But Satan wasn't satisfied. "But he *repented*," he said. "And he never—not even once—lost his faith. He really was a man after God's own heart."

"But you did get your foot in the door," they reminded him.

"Only my foot," he gloomed, "and God slammed the door on my toes."

They groused about that for a moment.

"Oh well," Satan finished, "perhaps we can do a better job on Solomon."

Checklist

Does God have it all together? Check it out and see:

1. God made a covenant with man.
2. Man blew it.
3. God called out a special NATION for Himself, and chose Abraham to be the father of it, and gave this nation THE PROMISED LAND.
4. God made a covenant with Abraham, gave him a son (Isaac) and promised to bless him if he would obey.
5. God tested Abraham's obedience; Abraham passed the test.
6. God appeared to Isaac's son Jacob and renewed the covenant promise again.
7. God led His NATION (Israel) to Egypt and left them there for 400 years so they could grow in numbers, then raised up Moses to lead them back again to THE PROMISED LAND.
8. God's nation (Israel) got to the very edge of the PROMISED LAND, and blew it again; they had to go back and wander in the wilderness for forty years.
9. Joshua finally led the Israelites over to the PROMISED LAND. They conquered it—*except for a few idols sprinkled here and there*.
10. The "few idols" grew into "many idols" and everyone in the nation "did his own thing." They finally demanded a king.
11. Now the NATION was a KINGDOM! With David (the second king) God renewed the covenant He had made with Adam way back in the garden of Eden, and promised that from *David's family* the Messiah would come—God would come to earth as a man.

CHAPTER 9

"BUT GOD, YOUR KINGDOM FELL APART."

"God, You Started Off Okay with Solomon—"

Now if Satan expected to do a job on Solomon, he was bitterly disappointed. A king never came to the throne with greater promise. For the first thing God did with Solomon was to tell him to ask for anything he wanted—

Anything—

And God would grant it.

"Ah, this is to my liking," thought Satan, "for here is where he falls on his face. He is bound to ask for riches, or for long life, or for power, or for—"

But Solomon asked for—

Of all things—

Wisdom.

"I can't believe it," said Satan, turning to his warlords. "Of all the things Solomon could have asked for, this is going to do me the most harm." He stared glumly into space. "Alas," he said, "this is going to be a long, up-hill battle. Solomon is *not* going to be easy to topple."

● ● ●

It was even worse than Satan had feared. God was so pleased with Solomon's request that He not only promised him wisdom, but He promised him wealth and long life to boot. And there began a reign such as Israel—indeed all the world—had never seen before.

Solomon built up an army of so many chariots and horses that he had to set aside whole cities to keep them. Silver and gold were as plentiful as rocks in the road!

And the Temple!

It was the most beautiful Temple the world had ever seen. The building of it required a force of 70,000 laborers and it took seven years.

Then he went on to build a most magnificent palace, which took 13 more years. He traded with the kings of all the surrounding nations. He made alliances with them.

Oh oh.

And he married their daughters to seal the bargains.[1]

"—Why Did He Blow It?"

"I'm beginning to see some hope for us," Satan said.

And he was right.

Solomon married the daughters of foreign kings until he had collected seven hundred wives. And each marriage made him richer.[2]

Then he began to build idol shrines so that his heathen wives might worship their heathen gods.

Then he began to amble over and worship with them.

Then he began to build *temples* for them.

Now all this high living meant that more and more workers were needed. And more money too. So Solomon drained his great empire for workers. And for money, in the form of high taxes. Until they had more than they could bear.

Slowly, surely, all this glory and all this wealth and greatness and power began to go down the drain. For Solomon was *no longer interested in the Lord God of Israel.*

He preferred to dabble in sin.

"God, Are You Really Finished This Time?"

God did not let Solomon dabble long.

First, God warned him but he didn't listen.

Then God *told* him, and the news wasn't good: After his death, his kingdom would be divided.[3]

"Bully!" Satan gloated, "Terrific!"

Part of the kingdom would be ruled by Solomon's son Rehoboam. And the other part would be ruled by Solomon's servant Jeroboam.

Jeroboam?!?

1. It was the custom in those days.
2. Read 2 Chronicles 9:22.
3. 1 Kings 11:11-13.

Who was *he*?
Why he was an overseer of one of Solomon's work forces!
Solomon was furious; surely, this young upstart had to go.
This young upstart *did* go.
Where?
To Egypt.
He fled for his life.
Now he was Solomon's *ex*-overseer.

"God, Your World Is Coming Apart at the Seams!"

After that, this great nation began to unravel and come apart. At the end, it happened rather quickly.

Solomon died.

His son Rehoboam was anointed king.

The people came to him and asked him to reduce their taxes and, while he was at it, to reduce their labor.

Rehoboam, heady with his new power, absolutely refused.

Meanwhile, Jeroboam returned from Egypt and he, being a very popular fellow, was promptly proclaimed king in the *northern* part of the kingdom.

And so the great nation of Israel was split in two.

Jeroboam (Solomon's ex-overseer) ruled the northern half (that was the large part) and retained the name of ISRAEL.

And Rehoboam (Solomon's son) ruled the southern half (that was the small part) and called it JUDAH.[4]

Now there were two wobbling nations in the place of one strong one.

Sorry business. Sorry business indeed.

"Guess Who Has His Foot in the Door—*Again*?"

But Satan's warlords were glum. "It's still one nation," they complained, "even though it's divided in two. What are you going to do about it?"

"Give me time," said Satan, "give me time. I'm working on it."

---

4. From here on out, God's people began to be called Jews also. First they were Hebrews, then Israelites. Remember?

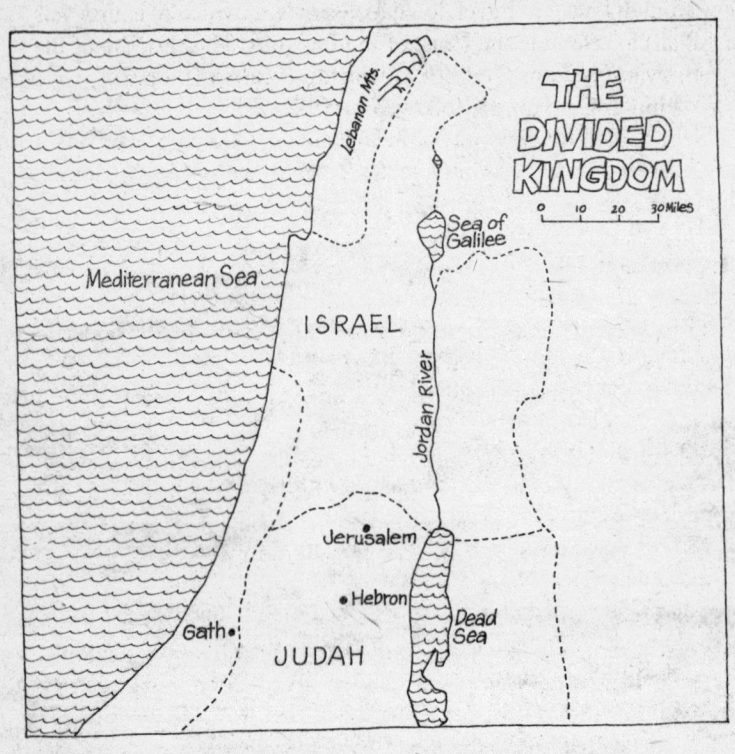

"What are you counting on?" they said.

"Well," said Satan, "Rehoboam is cocky and proud. I can always find a way to deal with people who are cocky and proud. Pride goes before destruction, you know, and a haughty spirit before a fall."[5]

"What of Jeroboam?" they wanted to know.

"We'll keep an eye on him," said Satan. "I'll find a way to deal with him."

"Jeroboam Is a Pushover, God."

Now Jeroboam proved to be easy to deal with. He wound up with *two golden calves* in his northern kingdom for the people to worship, so

5. See Proverbs 16:18.

they wouldn't have to travel down to Jerusalem (which of course was in Judah) to celebrate the Feast of the Passover. This, in spite of the solemn warning from God not to worship handmade idols!

And most of the people followed him blindly.

"See?" Satan told his warlords, "what did I tell you? He was a pushover. Just leave everything to me. I'll have the whole kingdom in shambles."

"Rehoboam *Too*."

Rehoboam was a little harder to handle—but not much.

He fortified Judah. The people were happy. For three wonderful years they followed the Lord God of Israel.

And then Rehoboam relaxed.

No time to worship.

And finally Rehoboam—and then his people—turned to idols again.

"We've nothing to worry about now," said Satan, "they're divided and their kings seem bent on leading them into idol worship. Things couldn't be better—for *us*."

"Israel Is on the Skids—"

Well, it certainly did look that way. Take Israel, for example. Eighteen kings after Jeroboam, she was still floundering, getting nowhere. For most of the kings had been bad.

The rest started out well enough—and then *turned* bad.

The end came with a king called Hoshea. He was neither hot nor cold; he was just wishy-washy.

Sargon the Second of Assyria was the one who finished Israel off. He captured the capital (Samaria) and the rest was just mopping-up operations. The people of Israel were taken in Assyria,

And Mesopotamia,

And Media.

They were scattered like buckshot all through the Assyrian empire.

It was thirteen hundred years after God had called a nation out for Himself, and had made that promise to Abraham. And now that nation was scattered, so it didn't seem possible that it could ever be gathered together again.

But wait.
There was still Judah left.

"—Judah Too?"

What of little Judah?

Well, out of twenty kings, Judah's score was pretty low. Not many of her kings were chaps you'd write home about. God was mostly forgotten. Even the beautiful Temple was neglected, filled with rubbish and deserted.

One of Judah's *good* kings (and they were rare) had it cleaned up one time. His name was Josiah. He had the rubbish taken out, and in the mess, the workmen found a scroll.

The laws of Moses!

The Word of God!

Josiah called the people from all over the land to come and worship.

They *did* come. And they repented before God. And they even celebrated the Feast of the Passover.

It was the first bright light that had shone through the darkness for many years.

But as time went on, that bright light flickered and went out, and the country was in darkness again.

Anyhow, Judah hung on for seven more kings, until Zedekiah.

He was the last one.

Now, if Zedekiah had been in the army, he would have been called Captain Anything. When all was going well, he listened to his advisors and false prophets.[6]

When he was frightened he sent for the prophet Jeremiah and asked what God had to say about the matter. And as soon as things would brighten a bit—

He'd go back to his false prophets again.

Meanwhile, King Nebuchadnezzar from Babylon struck at Jerusalem twice, carrying away captives and loot[7] each time, and, finally, like a lion leaping on its prey, crushed it altogether.

---

6. And were THEY ever a sorry lot!
7. That included all the furniture and the gold of the Temple.

And in the end, Zedekiah went along with thousands of prisoners being taken to Babylon.

Jerusalem was in flames.

Zedekiah stumbled along blindly, for they had poked out his eyes.

He was finished.

And so was Judah.

"God, They're *Wiped Out*. What Now?!?"

So the bright new nation that God had called out from all the people in the world, was WIPED OUT.

The ten tribes in the north were scattered to the ends of the earth, never to be heard of again.

And the *family* that God had called out of that nation had been in *Judah*. And now their descendants were being led away captive to Babylon.

All the great leaders God had raised up—

Abraham,

Isaac,

Jacob,

Moses,

Joshua,

Samuel,

David,

Had lived and died in vain. And everything was gone now.

Solomon's great Temple.

And all the wealth.

And all the glory.

Gone.

Surely God must be dead.

Or He had given up the whole thing.

Man wasn't worth it.

"God, You're Not Through with Those People Yet?"

Had things really gotten into such a mess that God didn't know how to straighten it out?

Not so, not so.

Don't forget God's covenant[8] with David.
So just hang in there.
It looks like God still had it all together.

Checklist

Does God really have it all together? Check it out and see:

1. God made a covenant with man.
2. Man blew it.
3. God called out a special NATION for Himself, and chose Abraham to be the father of it, and gave this nation THE PROMISED LAND.
4. God made a covenant with Abraham, gave him a son (Isaac) and promised to bless him if he would obey.
5. God tested Abraham's obedience; Abraham passed the test.
6. God appeared to Isaac's son Jacob and renewed the covenant promise again.
7. God led His NATION (Israel) to Egypt and left them there for 400 years so they could grow in numbers, then raised up Moses to lead them back again to THE PROMISED LAND.
8. God's nation (Israel) got to the very edge of the PROMISED LAND, and blew it again; they had to go back and wander in the wilderness for forty years.
9. Joshua finally led the Israelites over to the PROMISED LAND. They conquered it—*except for a few idols sprinkled here and there.*
10. The "few idols" grew into "many idols" and everyone in the nation "did his own thing." They finally demanded a king.
11. Now the NATION was a KINGDOM! With David (the second king) God renewed the covenant He had made with Adam way back in the garden of Eden, and promised that from *David's family* the Messiah would come—God would come to earth as a man, born as a baby.
12. The great new kingdom prospered, then turned to idol worship and was first divided (Israel and Judah), then conquered, and the Jews went into captivity—some of them disappeared altogether, some of them went to Babylon.

8. God's promise, remember?

CHAPTER 10

"GOD, CAN YOU STRAIGHTEN OUT THIS MESS?"

"But God, You Can't Keep Your Promise in *Babylon*."

Babylon!

The greatest, most powerful, most beautiful city in the ancient world!

It was famous for its temples and gardens and magnificent buildings—and Nebuchadnezzar's dazzling complex of palaces and the two enormous walls that surrounded it—and a hundred things more.

But something new had been added—thousands of Jews that Nebuchadnezzar had taken from Jerusalem!

He had taken the healthiest and the brainiest of them all. Within its great walls they lived. In its fields, and in its gardens and in its homes, they worked. And some of the very brainiest and choicest of them were even in the king's palace.

Daniel was one.

"God, You Mean You're Still on Speaking Terms with Your People?"

And God used Daniel for something of absolutely *earthshaking importance*.

God made it clear through Daniel that He not only knew what HAD been going on—
And what WAS going on—
BUT WHAT WAS GOING TO GO ON, IN THE FUTURE.
It all happened because of a dream.
King Nebuchadnezzar had the dream.
And God enabled Daniel to tell what it meant.

"God, Are You Speaking or Aren't You?"

It was a dream of a mighty image, dazzling in its brightness, frightening to look upon. Its head was gold—
Its breast and arms were silver—
Its belly and thighs were bronze—
Its legs were iron—
And its feet were part iron and part clay.
"You, O king," said Daniel, "are king above all kings on earth. *You are the head of gold.* The silver and bronze and iron and clay are the kingdoms that will come after you. They will be strong—but none as great as you are now. And then, and *then*—"
Yes, there was more to the dream, and it was very VERY important.[1]
But after all these predictions, what happened?
Nothing.
Ten years went by.
Twenty years, thirty, forty.
The Jews wept for their homeland in Jerusalem.
Fifty years went by.
Sixty, seventy.[2]

"Wow! Action at Last! And This Time—No Idols!"

And then Cyrus, the head of the great Medo-Persian empire came down upon the kingdom of Nebuchadnezzar—and conquered it!
Medo-Persia, the breast and arms of the image in Nebuchadnezzar's dream. The kingdom of silver!

1. You'll read about it later.
2. The prophet Jeremiah had *said* the Israelites would be in captivity for 70 years!

Astonishing!

Then Cyrus proceeded to do the very thing the prophet Isaiah had written that he would do, two hundred years before. Among other things, Isaiah had written, "I AM THE LORD that maketh all things . . . that saith of Cyrus, he shall perform all my pleasure: even saying to Jerusalem, thou shalt be built. . . ."[3]

Seem incredible?

Well, it really happened.

The Bible tells us that Cyrus issued a proclamation. He had it written down. And shouted from the housetops.

And it said: "The Lord hath charged me to build Him a house at Jerusalem . . . Who is there among you of His people? . . . Go up to Jerusalem . . . and build the house of the Lord."

Who was there among them who wanted to go?

Why Babylon was laced with faithful Israelites who had been waiting and praying for this very thing.

And off they went, with Cyrus' blessing—and with animals and gold and silver and all sorts of supplies. AND the sacred vessels of the Temple that had been stolen seventy years before.

When they finally got to Jerusalem, they set up shelters and dug in. And they built an altar and offered burnt offerings to the Lord.

It looked like old times.

At last—at long last, they were back on the right track again.

"This is ridiculous," said Satan to his warlords. "Inject into their minds the desire to worship idols again."

But the strangest thing had happened.

THE YEARS OF CAPTIVITY HAD CURED THE ISRAELITES FOREVER FROM WORSHIPING IDOLS!!![4]

Phew! At least THAT was over!

"God, Watch It—Satan Is Trying to Get His Foot in the Door Again."

"Well, then," said Satan. "Harass them, trouble them, bug them.

---

3. Read Isaiah 44:28; 45:1-4.
4. In their history, they have never been known to worship idols again, even to this very day!

Let their enemies do it. The Samaritans are living right around there. And there are other hostile neighbors; put them all to work!"

So Satan's warlords and demons got into a frenzy of activity to stop the building program.

But the Israelites were in a frenzy of activity too.

Not without their ups and downs, of course.

BUT NOT WITHOUT GOD EITHER.

"Bug them!" Satan bellowed, "So they'll get discouraged!"

They got discouraged, but the prophet Haggai spurred them on.

"Let them get chummy with their neighbors, marry them!" Satan ranted, "It has always worked before. It can work again!"

But when they intermarried with their neighbors, God sent them Ezra who told them to *seek the law of the Lord*.[5]

"I don't care if they intermarry or fight," Satan raved, "as long as they don't have time to *build*!"

But when their unfriendly neighbors wrote back to Persia, telling lies about them, and the king of Persia ordered all the work halted—God sent them the prophet, Nehemiah, who rolled up his sleeves and got busy. He organized them in round-the-clock shifts and, believe it or not, the walls of Jerusalem were built back up, strong as ever—

In fifty-two days!!!

And they got Ezra the priest to teach them a Bible lesson to boot![6]

And so, slowly, painfully, the Temple was restored and the walls were repaired and Jerusalem came crawling and limping out of its ashes.

"God, the Jews Are Back Home, but What a Mess!"

The Jews were back in their land. THE PROMISED LAND.

But any resemblance between their land now and their land under the marvelous rules of David and Solomon were purely coincidental.

Then—

"But Daniel's Dream Is Coming True!"

More of Nebuchadnezzar's dream came true!

5. See Ezra 7:10.
6. Nehemiah 8.

Alexander the Great of Greece conquered Persia, and the great Greek civilization took over—with Greek customs, Greek thinking, and especially *the Greek language*.

Now it was here.

The belly and thighs of Nebuchadnezzar's image—the kingdom of bronze!

"But God—It Does Seem as If Satan Has Won."

And the years rolled on.

And on.

And on.

There were no more prophets for Israel.

Malachi had been a prophet of God shortly after the walls were built. He had warned them about becoming indifferent and cold.

But if the Israelites had been rated on a scale from one to ten as to their warmth toward God, they probably would have rated a 2.5.

A hundred years.

Two hundred.

Three hundred.

FOUR HUNDRED.

In four hundred years, God had not spoken to them once. It did seem as if Satan had won.

And then—

More of Nebuchadnezzar's dream came true.

The legs—the legs of iron!

For the great ROMAN EMPIRE took possession of the whole works.

A rule of iron!

This was a different world now. A bigger world—a *much* bigger world. A hustling, bustling, busy world. The past glories were gone, and all the promises—

So much had happened. So many things had crowded it.

● ● ●

"Give them plenty of time to forget," said Satan. "In time it will all seem like a dream."

And indeed, to some it did. They went to the Temple and listened to the stories of Abraham and Isaac and Jacob and Moses—

And Daniel—

And that dream of Nebuchadnezzar's, so long long ago.

"God, Can the Stone in Daniel's Dream Be the *Messiah*?"

"You saw a mighty image," Daniel had said, "of gold and silver and bronze and iron, and then—"

There was more!

"Then you saw a stone come out of nowhere and crush the image, so that it was PULVERIZED and blew away!

"And the stone became a great mountain that filled the whole earth. And some day—"

THERE WAS MORE!

"Some day, God will set up a kingdom stronger than any kingdom made by man, and that kingdom *will never be destroyed*!"

The stone that filled the earth!

The kingdom that would never be destroyed!

Could that stone be the *Messiah* they had been promised from the beginning????

Could that stone be the *Saviour* they had all been looking for these many centuries?

"But God, Does Your Silence Mean You're Through at Last?"

Ah, but God had not spoken to them for four hundred years.

Not once, not one word.

Was it possible that the rest of the dream might come true? Was it possible that He would ever speak to them again?

• • •

"Not if I can help it," muttered Satan, his eyes glowing red.

Checklist
Does God still have it all together? Hang in there!

1. God made a covenant with man.
2. Man blew it.
3. God called out a special NATION for Himself, and chose Abraham to be the father of it, and gave the nation THE PROMISED LAND.
4. God made a covenant with Abraham, gave him a son (Isaac) and promised to bless him if he would obey.
5. God tested Abraham's obedience; Abraham passed the test.
6. God appeared to Isaac's son Jacob and renewed the covenant promise again.
7. God led His NATION (Israel) to Egypt and left them there for 400 years so they could grow in numbers, then raised up Moses to lead them back again to THE PROMISED LAND.
8. God's nation (Israel) got to the very edge of the PROMISED LAND, and blew it again; they had to go back and wander in the wilderness for forty years.
9. Joshua finally led the Israelites over to the PROMISED LAND. They conquered it—*except for a few idols sprinkled here and there.*
10. The "few idols" grew into "many idols" and everyone in the nation "did his own thing." They finally demanded a king.
11. Now the NATION was a KINGDOM! With David (the second king) God renewed the covenant He had made with Adam way back in the garden of Eden, and promised that from *David's family* the Messiah would come—God would come to earth as a man, born as a baby.
12. The great new kingdom prospered, then turned to idol worship and was first divided (Israel and Judah), then conquered, and the Jews went into captivity—some of them disappeared altogether, some of them went to Babylon.
13. In Babylon, God revealed to His prophet Daniel what was to come, right up to the end of times!

But then—four hundred years of silence!

PART TWO

CHAPTER 11

"GOD, YOU MEAN THE MESSIAH YOU PROMISED IS *JESUS*?"

"God, What in the World Is Going On?"

Four hundred years of silence!

And the Israelites were *still* waiting for the Messiah.

After four hundred years, what in the world was going on?

Well, for one thing,

Roman rule was everywhere.[1] From the Atlantic Ocean to the Caspian Sea. And from Britain to the Nile River.

One vast empire.

And Caesar was the ruler in power.

And for another thing,

The Greek language was known everywhere. Though each "province" had its own language and spoke its own native tongue—

Everybody spoke Greek.

And for *another* thing,

The whole empire was laced with those famous Roman roads you've read about in your history books. Which made travel easy.

So the whole empire was like one vast neighborhood. News could get around.

NEWS COULD GET AROUND!

So if—*if* the Messiah *did* come—why the good news could explode in all directions!

But after four hundred years of silence, would the Messiah come?

And if He did—

Where?

And how?

---

1. The iron legs in Nebuchadnezzar's dream, remember?

"God, You Mean the Jews Are Still Waiting for the Messiah?"

Zacharias was going about his work in the Temple, in Jerusalem. He performed his duties as he had performed them many, many times before.

Zacharias was very old. He lived up in a little village in the hills of Judea, south of Jerusalem. He was staying in Jerusalem only for the week, for it was the week his division was on duty. And it was a very special week for him, for only one priest was allowed in the inner sanctuary to burn incense before the Lord. They drew lots to see who it would be—and this week the honor had fallen to him.

He went into the inner sanctuary and walked toward the Altar of Incense. Outside the Temple he could hear the great crowd praying, as they always did during that part of the service.

Then suddenly—

An *angel*!

"God, You're Speaking Again—At Last!"

An angel standing to the right of the Altar of Incense!

Now Zacharias had never even *seen* an angel before. And this one was *talking* to him. Old Zacharias was rooted to the spot with terror.

"Don't be afraid," the angel said. "I've come to tell you that your wife Elizabeth will bear you a son. He will be like the prophet Elijah, a man of power, and he will prepare the people for the arrival of the Messiah."

Zacharias had been waiting all his life for some word from God. And when he finally heard it, he couldn't believe it!

He found his voice at last.

"God, This Man Is Not a Very Good Risk."

But what he said would never go down in history as one of the great speeches of faith.

"It's impossible," he babbled, "My wife and I are too old."

Good grief.

Well, the angel didn't argue with him. "I am Gabriel," he said. "I stand in the presence of God. It was God Himself who sent me to you

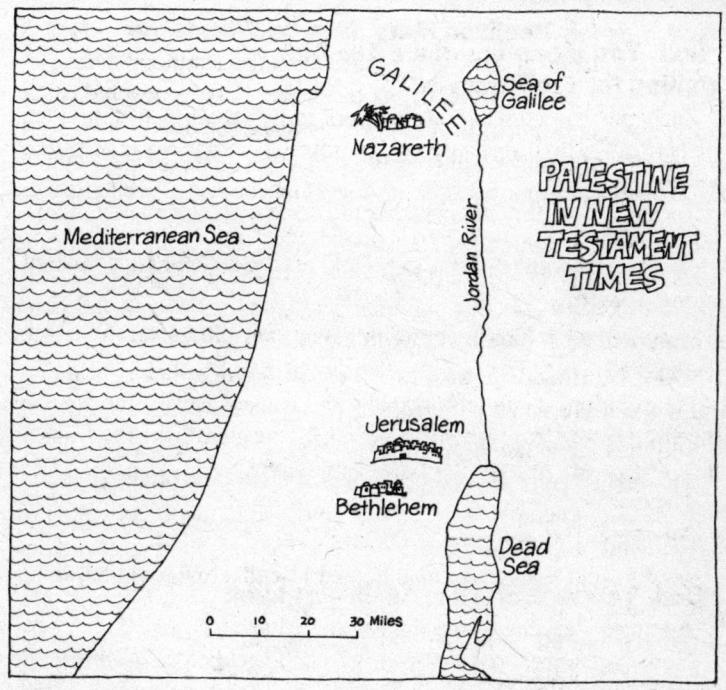

with this news. And you can't believe it? Then you are to be struck dumb until it comes true—until the child is born."

And then the angel was gone.

"But Aren't You a Little Rough on Him?"

Outside, the crowd stirred restlessly, wondering why the old priest didn't come out. Inside, Zacharias wondered how he was going to be *able* to walk out. At the moment he was wondering what was even holding him up, he was so frightened.

When he finally did go out and face the crowd, he realized the angel really had been there. And really had spoken. And really meant what he said.

For Zacharias tried to talk.

And he couldn't.

"God, I Never Realized Mary Was So Wonderful . . ."

The little town of Nazareth nestled into the southern ranges of lower Galilee. Just a spot on the map, a hokey town you would call it today, not worth much. In that town lived a girl named Mary, who was of no importance either—*except that she was a descendant of David*. And a few months after the angel Gabriel visited Zacharias, *he visited Mary*.

"The Lord is with you," the angel told her. "You are highly favored among women."

Mary looked at him in confusion. Whatever did he mean?

"Don't be afraid," he went on, "You are going to have a son and you will call His name JESUS."

And then came the thunderbolt.

"He shall be great. He will be the Son of God—and of His kingdom there will be no end."

The child of God?

But she was engaged to a man named Joseph. How could this thing be?

"How could this thing be?" she asked aloud.

"The Holy Spirit of God shall come upon you, and the power of God shall overshadow you. So the baby born to you will be utterly holy—the Son of God."[2]

Mary considered this very carefully in her heart. This was a complete and total commitment.[3]

And then, finally, "Let it be done to me as you have said," she whispered.

Now to believe it herself was one matter; to tell all this to Joseph was quite another.

But God had already thought of that. For an angel appeared to Joseph in a dream and told *him* not to be afraid. Mary's baby would be the Son of God.[4]

2. See Luke 1:26-35.
3. It means "I give You my life, God—*all* of it."
4. See Matthew 1:22,23.

A few months later, Zacharias and his wife had their son, just as the angel Gabriel had promised. And during the circumcision ceremony, with the whole neighborhood around as witnesses, the unbelievable happened.

Naturally, the guests asked the parents what the child's name would be, and naturally they assumed it would be Zacharias, after his father.

And Zacharias wrote on a pad "His name is John."

Then suddenly there was no longer any need for the writing pad. For Zacharias, right on the spot, got his voice back!

First he told his listeners about his conversation with Gabriel, how he had been struck dumb because he hadn't believed God.

Then he dropped a bombshell:

This child, when he grew up, would be a prophet, and his whole purpose for being born, and his whole purpose in life, would be to announce the coming of the Messiah!

Zacharias' silence of months had finally been broken. But more important, the silence of God, which had lasted for four hundred years, had been broken too.

The Messiah was coming—at last!!!

"God, You Mean the Messiah You Promised Is *JESUS*?"

Well you can believe that Satan and his warlords were watching all this with avid[5] interest. Could this child that had been promised to Mary, actually be the Messiah? For the promise was that the Messiah would be born in Bethlehem. And Joseph and Mary lived in *Nazareth*.

How was God going to work that one out?

They didn't have long to wait.

"Yes God, How *Are* You Going to Work This One Out?"

God works things out in mysterious ways, and hardly ever twice the same. Sometimes He works through miracles. Sometimes He works through ordinary people. Sometimes He works through leaders. Even

---

5. With their ears hanging out!

kings play into His hands without even realizing what they are doing. For, a few months later, a most unexpected thing happened.

Caesar decided to take a census.

Everyone had to go back to his own hometown and register. And where was Joseph's hometown?

You guessed it.

Bethlehem.

So Joseph and Mary made the trek to Bethlehem and braved the traffic jams and the donkeys and the camels and the crowds and the carriages and the caravans—

But you know the story well.

When they got there—there were more people than accommodations. The inns were booked solid. And they had to stay in a cave where the animals were kept.

And there, in the cave, Mary's baby was born.

She wrapped Him in a blanket and laid Him in a manger.[6]

"But God, It's the Most Important Birth Announcement in the World. Shouldn't You Announce It from the Temple?"

And outside of town, the angels announced it to a few lonely shepherds watching their sheep by night: "For unto you this day is born a Savior which is Christ the Lord."

Born where?

"In the city of David."

In the very city where David had been born—David's own hometown![7]

• • •

"I'm really not worried," said Satan (in a worried voice). "No one will find out about it. It hasn't been shouted from the housetops. It hasn't been announced from kings' palaces. Who knows about it? Only a few lowly shepherds watching their sheep by night. Who can they tell? And if they do tell, who will believe them?"

6. See Luke 2:7.
7. Remember God's contract with David on page 67?

"God, It's Not a Very Good Beginning."

Well, indeed it *didn't* look like a very good beginning.

What happened?

Nothing.

Time went by. Joseph and Mary moved into a house there in Bethlehem. And the infant Jesus grew to be a small child.

Then, out of the blue—

Wise men appeared from the East, to ask where this new *King* was. They had seen His star, they said, and had made the long journey from way back in Persia.

• • •

Satan's warlords jumped to attention. "These wise men have gone to Herod himself to inquire after this new King of the Jews," they reported to him, "and Herod has questioned them about this new King. And has asked them to report to him when they found this child so that he may worship him too. That's bad."

"No, that's good," said Satan. "The last thing Herod wants is another king. Why he's murdered half his own family already, for fear that one of them would take his throne. He wants the child *killed*."

"And so do we," they answered.

"Exactly. Patience, patience, he'll do our work for us, he'll do it well."

• • •

Well the wise men did find the child Jesus.

BUT.

They were warned in a dream by God *not to go back and tell Herod*, but to go back to their home in the East by a different route.

Which they did.

And *Joseph* was warned in a dream to take Mary and the child Jesus and go hide in Egypt until the storm blew over.

Which *he* did.

Phew! *That* was close!

Mary and Joseph did not return until Herod's death. And then they moved to Nazareth to settle down and live.

• • •

Satan was consumed with a raging hatred.

"But Jesus is living in obscurity,[8] in Nazareth," his warlords tried to comfort him.

"Keep it that way," hissed Satan. "In the meantime, there are others to work on. Work on the priests and the Temple leaders. Get them on a power trip. Fill them full of self-righteousness.[9] Make them substitute a list of 'dos and don'ts' for God."

Yes, there were all kinds of things they could do.

"Harden their hearts," Satan went on. "Dull their brains."

Ah, good idea.

"They're expecting a king? Well, tell them to expect a king who will come in like a whirlwind to deliver them from the Romans."

Bully!

"This child, when He grows up—*if* He grows up—will be a peasant. They won't give Him a second look."

All *right*!

"Get to work on it!" he shrieked, "we don't have much time!"

Right on!!!

Satan's warlords got to work, all right, but there was nothing left but mopping-up operations. The VIPs[10] in the Temple were already so self-righteous there was not much left to do. They had been going through the motions of worshiping God in their own prescribed way for so long, they had "jelled" that way.

And so the years went by.

Enough years for two baby boys to grow up to be men.

John the Baptist.

And JESUS.

Checklist

Does God have it all together? Check it out and see:

8. Nobody knows He's around.
9. I'm okay. I don't need God.
10. Very Important People.

1. God made a covenant with man.

2. Man blew it.

3. God called out a special NATION for Himself, and chose Abraham to be the father of it, and gave this nation THE PROMISED LAND.

4. God made a covenant with Abraham, gave him a son (Isaac) and promised to bless him if he would obey.

5. God tested Abraham's obedience; Abraham passed the test.

6. God appeared to Isaac's son Jacob and renewed the covenant promise again.

7. God led His NATION (Israel) to Egypt and left them there for 400 years so they could grow in numbers, then raised up Moses to lead them back again to THE PROMISED LAND.

8. God's nation (Israel) got to the very edge of the PROMISED LAND, and blew it again; and they had to go back and wander in the wilderness for forty years.

9. Joshua finally led the Israelites over to the PROMISED LAND. They conquered it—*except for a few idols sprinkled here and there.*

10. The "few idols" grew into "many idols" and everyone in the nation "did his own thing." They finally demanded a king.

11. Now the NATION was a KINGDOM! With David (the second king) God renewed the covenant He had made with Adam way back in the garden of Eden, and promised that from *David's family* the Messiah would come—God would come to earth as a man, born as a baby.

12. The great new kingdom prospered, then turned to idol worship and was first divided (Israel and Judah), then conquered, and the Jews went into captivity—some of them disappeared altogether, some of them went to Babylon.

13. In Babylon, God revealed to His prophet Daniel what was to come, right up to the end of times!

But then—four hundred years of silence!

14. Four hundred years later, when the world had grown ENORMOUS and was under Roman rule—God renewed His promise to MARY (who was a descendant of David!). And in David's hometown (Bethlehem) the Messiah was born. And His name was JESUS.

CHAPTER 12

"GOD, ISN'T ANYBODY LISTENING?"

"God, the People Are Only Half Listening—"

"Repent!!!"

What was *this*?

"Repent! For the Kingdom of Heaven is at hand!!!"

What?!?

The cry came from the craggy rocks and the dry stubble of the desert, from a man whose garments were of camel's hair. From a man who was a health food nut, no less—he ate nothing but locusts and wild honey. He preached with a fire and enthusiasm that sent people scurrying from all directions into the desert to hear him.

They listened to him, frightened. "Who are you?" they said.

"I am not the Messiah," he answered, for he knew that's what they thought.

"But who, then? Are you Elijah?"

"No."

"Who, then?"

Who, indeed?

"—And the Leaders Aren't Listening at All."

The VIPs of the Temple wondered too. Why this young upstart was even baptizing people in the River Jordan. He was beginning to collect a group of followers. And every day it got bigger. He might be dangerous; they had better go see for themselves.

They went out, their pompous heads high, their noses in the air, their beards bristling. They went out to give him a lacing. But instead of that, he gave *them* one.

He compared them with the snakes that scurry out of their cracks during a desert fire, and flee for safety.

"And who warned *you* to flee from the wrath to come?" he cried.

"Us?" they sputtered.

"Yes, YOU," he warned, "you sons of snakes. Don't think you're safe because you're descendants of Abraham! I am the voice of one crying in the wilderness, make straight the way of the *Lord*."

Their beards quivered with rage.

"Yes, I am baptizing in the River Jordan," he went on. "But someone else is coming, far greater than I am. So great that I am not worthy to carry His shoes. And *He* will baptize you with the Holy Spirit and with fire!"

What?!?

This man was proclaiming the coming of the Messiah! Was he for real?

"God, He's Talking About Jesus. Is Man Going to Blow It Again?"

He was for real, all right. For this was John, the son who had been promised to the priest Zacharias. *John the Baptist*.

And he was doing what God had sent him upon earth to do.

Yes.

John was talking about Jesus.

Jesus, who had been there when the world had been created. Jesus, who had come down as the "angel of the Lord" and had spoken to Abraham.

And Isaac.

And Jacob.

And Moses.

And Joshua.

And David and Solomon and all the prophets, down through the ages.

For at last—at long last—the Messiah God had promised from the very beginning, was here!
JESUS!

Checklist

Has God got it all together? Check it out and see:

1. God made a covenant with man.
2. Man blew it.
3. God called out a special NATION for Himself, and chose Abraham to be the father of it, and gave this nation THE PROMISED LAND.
4. God made a covenant with Abraham, gave him a son (Isaac) and promised to bless him if he would obey.
5. God tested Abraham's obedience; Abraham passed the test.
6. God appeared to Isaac's son Jacob and renewed the covenant promise again.
7. God led His NATION (Israel) to Egypt and left them there for 400 years so they could grow in numbers, then raised up Moses to lead them back again to THE PROMISED LAND.
8. God's nation (Israel) got to the very edge of the PROMISED LAND, and blew it again; they had to go back and wander in the wilderness for forty years.
9. Joshua finally led the Israelites over to the PROMISED LAND. They conquered it—*except for a few idols sprinkled here and there.*
10. The "few idols" grew into "many idols" and everyone in the nation "did his own thing." They finally demanded a king.
11. Now the NATION was a KINGDOM! With David (the second king) God renewed the covenant He had made with Adam way back in the garden of Eden, and promised that from *David's family* the Messiah would come—God would come to earth as a man, born as a baby.
12. The great new kingdom prospered, then turned to idol worship and was first divided (Israel and Judah), then conquered, and the Jews went into captivity—some of them disappeared altogether, some of them went to Babylon.

13. In Babylon, God revealed to His prophet Daniel what was to come, right up to the end of times!

But then—four hundred years of silence!

14. Four hundred years later, when the world had grown ENORMOUS and was under Roman rule—God renewed His promise to MARY (who was a descendant of David!) And in David's hometown (Bethlehem) the Messiah was born. And His name was Jesus!

15. John the Baptist told the people that JESUS the MESSIAH was here at last!

CHAPTER 13

"BUT GOD, JESUS IS HERE. DOESN'T ANYBODY CARE?"

"God, a *Few* Seem to Care."

The banks of the Jordan were crowded.

People had come from all the towns everywhere to hear this prophet, John the Baptist, preach.

"Turn from your sins!" he kept crying. "Turn to God!"

Now clearly, words like that called for a decision.

Turn *from*.

And turn *to*.

And some of them made that decision in their hearts. They *wanted* to turn to God. And as a sign that they wanted to turn to God, they came to John, at the River Jordan, to be baptized.

"God, You Mean JESUS Has to Make a Choice?"

And then one day—

Jesus Himself stepped forth from the crowd and walked down toward the water. To be *baptized*? *Jesus*?

Yes.

Now, this startled nobody because He was only the carpenter's son—the son of Joseph and Mary. It startled nobody but John the Baptist himself. For he knew who Jesus really was.

The Son of God.
Not only the crowd was watching.
All heaven was watching.
And Satan and his warlords were watching too.

"He has two ways to go," said Satan. "He can set up His kingdom on earth, and be a king here and now. Or He can carry out God's plan.[1] We'll have to wait and see. Perhaps we can help Him decide."

Jesus walked into the water toward John. And John instinctively wanted to back away. "It isn't proper," he said, "I'm the one who needs to be baptized by *You*."

"And He's Choosing *Man*?"

"Please," said Jesus, "Just do it. For I must do all that is right."

And John, in fear and trembling, baptized Jesus, the Son of God. There was no one in the crowd that day who realized what was really happening except John the Baptist and Jesus.

And then a most amazing thing took place.

As soon as Jesus came up out of the water—

The heavens opened. The Holy Spirit of God came down in the form of a dove. And then a voice from heaven said, "This is My beloved Son in whom I am well pleased"!

No one else saw or heard.
Only Jesus.
And John.
Oh.

And Satan too. He turned to his warlords. And he let out a long hiss like that of a goose. "He has chosen to carry out God's plan," he said. "He's going to identify Himself with man."

And so God, for a few brief years, was also man. This is the great mystery of the ages.

"Watch It, God—Satan Is Up to Something."

"We've bungled everything," muttered Satan. "He has done it. Under our very noses, He has done it. He is now identified with man,

---

1. That Jesus would die to save us from our sins.

and He intends to carry out His plan. The only thing we can do is to try to mess it up."

They nodded in approval.

"I am not finished yet," he said. "Let's get going."

• • •

Between Jerusalem and the Dead Sea was a wilderness of sand and crumbling limestone—hot and dry and incredibly lonely. It was there that Jesus went next, to be alone with God and to think out this great task that God had put before Him. He had no food. And no water.

"No more bungling," said Satan. "We can't afford it. I'll handle this one myself."

"Are you going to attack Him personally?" they said.

"I'm going to attack Him through His mind," said Satan. "By suggestion. I'm going to *tempt* Him."

And he did.

"Why wait," he said to Jesus, "to prove that you are the Son of God? Command these stones to be turned into loaves of bread. That will prove it."

"No," Jesus answered. "The Scriptures tell us that men don't live by bread alone—but by obedience to every word of God."

One down.

Satan tried again. This time he appealed to pride. "Why wait?" he said. "Why not take a shortcut? Prove your power now. Jump off the pinnacle of the Temple—four hundred feet! If you're the Son of God, His angels will bear you up. You can astonish people into following you. It would be easy."

"The Scriptures also say 'Don't put God to a foolish test!' " answered Jesus.

Two down.

Satan tried again.

Now if there was one thing Satan wanted more than anything on earth, it was to be *worshiped*. It was the cause of his fall in the first place, way back there at the beginning of the world. It was his consuming desire.

Next, he took Jesus in a vision to the peak of a high mountain, and showed Him the nations of the world. "I am the prince of this world," he said, "and I'll give it all to you *now*—if You'll only kneel and worship me. Why wait? You can have it *now*. Just for *one moment*, worship me. *Kneel and worship me*."

There was a great silence as if all heaven and all hell were waiting for Jesus' answer.

"Jesus *Has* Chosen Man!"

Jesus gave it in four words.

"*Get-out-of-here*."

And then He added, "The Scriptures say, 'Worship only the Lord God. Obey ONLY HIM.' "[2]

Wow! Whoooeeeee! And Hallelujah!

It was over!

Satan *got*.

Reeeeeal fast.

Jesus had made His choice. He would go the way God had chosen from the beginning of the world, and that way was the way of the cross. From then on He began to preach, "Turn from sin, and turn to God, for the Kingdom of Heaven is here."

"But Satan Isn't Giving Up."

Satan went back to his warlords in defeat. "There is only one way to tell this and that is to tell it straight out," he told them.

"What happened?" they said.

"He clobbered me. He *pulverized* me with the Word of God. God is going to carry out His plan."

"Isn't there anything we can do?" they said.

"We can delay it," he said. "I want—" and his voice grew strong; he was beginning to recover—"I want such an outpouring of demon activity as has not been seen since this world began. I want a concentration of demons in this area—a *huge* concentration."

"Right, master," they said. "Anything else?"

"You might work on the religious leaders," he said. "Make them

---

2. Read Matthew 4:1-11.

'holier-than-thou,'[3] more than ever before. I want their list of 'dos and don'ts' so long it will stretch from here to Rome and back. And dull their minds so that they will not hear the truth."

"Yes master. Right on! Anything else?"

"No, that's the best we can do at the moment," he said. "Get going!"

"But God—Satan Is Finding All the Weak Links. Aren't You in Trouble Again?"

Meanwhile, Jesus was collecting His disciples. There were twelve of them. "Let's see what we have here," said Satan. And he checked over the list. "Peter, eh? Very explosive chap. He has a big mouth. See that every time he opens it, he puts his foot in it."

"Yes, sire," they said. "Peter. Big mouth. Foot. Right on."

"James and John," Satan muttered, going down the list. "Brothers. Sons of Zebedee. Short-tempered, I believe, both of them. They'll do very well. Then there's Andrew, sort of a dust-eater. Stays behind in the shadow. And Philip, there's another good one. Very timid chap. And Matthew. A tax collector. That's good, that's good. And Thomas. Filled with doubts, believes only what he can see. And there's James and Thaddeus and Simon. Very good. I note that not one of these men is schooled in the rabbinical law.[4] Have fairly decent educations but they're all laymen, everyone. Very second-rate, *very* second-rate. That's good."

Well, it was true. Peter *was* explosive. (But so was Jacob, remember?) James and John had tempers. (But so did Moses on occasion.) Andrew was very quiet, and a second banana. (But so was Joshua.) Philip was timid. (But so was Gideon.) And so on, down the list. Not one of them was perfect, not one. (But not one of God's leaders ever *was*.)

"Satan Is Powerful—"

Meanwhile, Satan kept his promise. The demon activity that was in the world was greater than it had ever been since the world began.

---

3. "I'm better than you are. I *do* do this, and I *don't* do that."
4. They weren't trained to be ministers or teachers or anything like that.

"—But Jesus Is More-So!"

Jesus ministered to the multitudes. He sought out the people where they were—in the synagogues, on the city streets, by the wayside, in the meadows and on the mountainside. He told them about the love of God. He told them about Himself; He healed the sick and He cast out demons. He knew the demons; He called them by name and forbade them to speak. Satan was indeed the prince of this world but his power went *only as far as Jesus would let it go*.

"God, Doesn't *Anybody* Have It Straight About Who Jesus Is?"

Then He began to draw His disciples aside and teach them by themselves. But they didn't realize that He was giving them a crash course in all the things that they would need to know *after He was gone*.

That was the whole point.

They did not, could not, believe that He would die. He told them all patiently, again and again, that He would die. And that God would raise Him up again. But the whole idea was too heavy for them. They couldn't handle it. He was going to set up a kingdom right here on earth *right* then, they kept telling themselves.

• • •

Satan's warlords had done a very good job on the Pharisees.[5]

"Who does this fellow think He is?" they cried. Was He claiming to be God? If He *wasn't* God, where did His strange power come from? "He casts out demons by the power of Satan!"[6] they bellowed.

"God, *Satan* Sure Knows!"

Satan chuckled at that one. "Good. Let them think that. Total confusion, that's what I like, total confusion."

But the crowds roared, "Maybe Jesus is the Messiah!"

"No matter, no matter," chuckled Satan, "I don't care what they call

---

5. The religious leaders, remember?
6. See Matthew 9:34.

Him—anything from an upstart to the devil. Or they can even call Him the Messiah. Just so long as they don't find out the truth."

"But God—Everybody Else Is All Mixed Up!"

The truth was not *only* that Jesus was the Messiah. The truth was that He was the Messiah *who had come to die.*

In spite of all He had done, all He had said, nobody, but nobody really understood this.

The religious leaders thought He was a fraud.[7]

The disciples thought He was the Messiah who had come to set up His kingdom right then and there, and free them from the Roman rule.

The crowds thought He was a miracle-worker, giving them bread and healing their diseases.

And the children? They just plain *loved* Him. They struggled through the crowds to get near Him. They wanted to touch Him, to listen to Him. Their love for Him was pure and clean. And perhaps that pleased God in heaven more than any grown-up's love could ever please Him, for the children wanted nothing in return except His love for them.

But even the children did not understand why He was there.

Toward the end of His stay on earth, He said:

"My light will shine out for you
Just a little while longer;
Walk in it
While you can;
Go where you want to go
Before the darkness falls,
For then it will be too late for you to find your way."

Checklist

Has God got it all together? Check it out and see:
 1. God made a covenant with man.
 2. Man blew it.

---

7. A phony.

3. God called out a special NATION for Himself, and chose Abraham to be the father of it, and gave this nation THE PROMISED LAND.

4. God made a covenant with Abraham, gave him a son (Isaac) and promised to bless him if he would obey.

5. God tested Abraham's obedience; Abraham passed the test.

6. God appeared to Isaac's son Jacob and renewed the covenant promise again.

7. God led His NATION (Israel) to Egypt and left them there for 400 years so they could grow in numbers, then raised up Moses to lead them back again to THE PROMISED LAND.

8. God's nation (Israel) got to the very edge of the PROMISED LAND, and blew it again; they had to go back and wander in the wilderness for forty years.

9. Joshua finally led the Israelites over to the PROMISED LAND. They conquered it—*except for a few idols sprinkled here and there.*

10. The "few idols" grew into "many idols" and everyone in the nation "did his own thing." They finally demanded a king.

11. Now the NATION was a KINGDOM! With David (the second king) God renewed the covenant He had made with Adam way back in the garden of Eden, and promised that from *David's family* the Messiah would come—God would come to earth as a man, born as a baby.

12. The great new kingdom prospered, then turned to idol worship and was first divided (Israel and Judah), then conquered, and the Jews went into captivity—some of them disappeared altogether, some of them went to Babylon.

13. In Babylon, God revealed to His prophet Daniel what was to come, right up to the end of times!

But then—four hundred years of silence!

14. Four hundred years later, when the world had grown ENORMOUS and was under Roman rule—God renewed His promise to MARY (who was a descendant of David!). And in David's hometown (Bethlehem) the Messiah was born. And His name was Jesus!

15. John the Baptist told the people that JESUS the MESSIAH was here at last!

16. God had come to earth as a person at last—to keep that promise He'd made to Adam. God loved men so much—*He* was going to pay the ransom and buy man back and deliver him from the slavery of sin, into the freedom of belonging to HIM!

CHAPTER 14

"THE RANSOM IS PAID, GOD—ARE YOU GOING TO GIVE MAN A CHOICE *AGAIN*?"

"God, the Promised Land Is the Same Land—"
And now it was Passover week again in Jerusalem.

The stage was set in the same land where God had led Abraham many, many years ago.

The same land where Isaac had wandered—

And Jacob had run away from Esau.

The same land that Joshua had conquered—

And the judges and then the kings had ruled.

Where God had made a covenant with David—

And Solomon had ruled in splendor.

Where the kingdom had been divided—

And the people had been carried off into captivity.

And finally, where they had come back to try again.

THE PROMISED LAND!

These were not a lot of separate events. This was ONE GREAT CONTINUED DRAMA of God's great plan for man!!!

"And the Passover Feast Is the Same Feast—"
The whole countryside around Jerusalem was crowded. And inside Jerusalem? Wall-to-wall people! Every adult male who lived within twenty miles *had* to come to the Passover. The Jews from every corner of the earth made their way there whether they had to come or not.

And brought their families.

And lambs.

There were thousands of them—one for each family.

The small families doubled up. There had to be a lamb for every ten people.

And so the people streamed in and bedded down wherever they could find lodging and got ready for the greatest week in all the year.

"—But the Passover *Lamb* Is Different!"

They didn't know it, but in God's great plan, there would never again be any need to kill a lamb.

And they didn't realize it, but *the real Passover Lamb was in Bethany*.

Jesus.

"God, What Is Jesus Up To?"

He had stayed with His friends there. And He'd made arrangements for them to get Him a donkey that had never been ridden before, so He could ride into Jerusalem.

And into Jerusalem He went, through the Golden Gate.

Into the Temple area.

He went riding in like a king.

Would He set up His kingdom? And rescue the Israelites from the hated Roman rule?

Was He the Messiah?

Was He really?

"He is the Messiah!" The crowds began to shout.

"Hosanna! Hosanna!"

Then, "Save us now!" It became a shout.

"Save us NOW—Save us NOW!" And their voices rose to the very heavens.

"What Is *Satan* Up To?"

"They want to make Him king *now*," said Satan. "And to set up His kingdom here and *now*."

"Will He do it?" his warlords said.

"No," he said. "Within a week they'll be wanting to kill Him. The chief priests and Pharisees would like to arrest Him now, but they don't dare. He's too popular. He will have to be betrayed into their hands—privately."

"How will all this be done?" they wanted to know.

"I'll see to it," said Satan, "through one of His disciples."

"One of His *disciples*?"

"Yes. Judas. I've been getting him set up for it for a long time."

"Will you use one of us?"

"No. It's too important. It must not fail. I'll do it myself."

"God, the Disciples Sure Don't Have It All Together!"

Jesus stayed in the Temple area in Jerusalem for only a short time and then left with His friends and went back to Bethany.

He came back the next day.

And the next.

And taught in the Temple as He had been doing.

And He told His disciples much of what was going to happen in the future.

His disciples listened to Him without really hearing. They still could not get it out of their heads that He was going to set up His kingdom then and there. And their main concern was whether they would have important positions in it!

"Is There Something Special About This Passover?"

Then at last came the day of the Passover.

All over Jerusalem, and all around Jerusalem, families were inside,[1] shut away from the cold evening air. The odor of roast lamb and herbs filled the air everywhere. And, while the people ate, they remembered that first Passover back in Egypt, so many, many years ago, when the blood of the lamb was sprinkled on the doorposts of the Israelites' homes to save them from punishment.

"There *Is* Something Special About This Passover!"

Somewhere in Jerusalem, upstairs in a borrowed room, Jesus and His disciples gathered around a low table to eat the Passover supper.

---

1. Inside homes, rented rooms, tents—wherever they'd been able to find shelter for the Passover week.

They would never eat together again, never on this earth.
   It was the last time.
   None of them realized it.
   Even after Jesus told them, they didn't believe it.
   He told them again[2] that He would have to suffer and die. And that one of them right there in that very room would betray Him.
   "Which one?"
   "Which one?"
   "Me, Lord?"
   "Is it I, Lord?"
   "*Who*??"

• • •

Satan had already entered into Judas.
Even as the disciples were talking, Judas hurried out into the night, along the dark chilly streets—
   To the house of the High Priest.
   He was on his way to betray Jesus, to turn Him in.
   He pulled his cloak more tightly around him.
   It was cold.

• • •

Upstairs in that borrowed room, Jesus took a small piece of bread. And He blessed it.
   And then He broke it in pieces.
   And He gave each one of them a piece.
   "Take it," He said, "And eat it. This is My body given for you."
   They sat staring at Him. Whatever did He mean?
   And then He took a cup of wine.
   And He gave it to them to pass around and drink from it.
   "This is My blood," He said. "It will be poured out so God can *pass over*[3] the sins of multitudes of people."
   They ate the bread and drank the wine, wondering.

2. He had told them before, many times.
3. Forgive!

What *did* He mean? It had always been a *lamb's* blood from the very beginning.

It was a *lamb's* blood way back in Egypt and it had been a *lamb's* blood ever since.

And even though, three years before, John the Baptist had pointed to Jesus and cried out "Behold the Lamb of God," they did not realize that He—that Jesus Himself—*was the Passover Lamb*.

"God, Is This What You Were Up To All the Time?"

They went from there up to the Mount of Olives and into a garden called Gethsemane.

It was there that Jesus had a long talk with His Father in heaven.

And all heaven waited, and all hell, and all creation.

And finally, "Whatever You want Me to do," Jesus said to His Father, "Your will be done."

And so the choice was made.

That was the night that Judas betrayed Him. And that was the night He was arrested and taken to the Chief Priest for an all-night session behind closed doors.

It was a night of horror.

He was turned over to the Sanhedrin.[4]

And hustled off to Pilate.

And then to king Herod.

And back to Pilate again.[4]

And the next day He was taken outside the city to a hill called the Skull—

And crucified.

And the punishment for all the sins that had ever *been* committed, or ever would *be* committed, was taken by—

God Himself!

For God had come to earth in the form of a man and that man was Jesus.

They called Him the Son of God.

He often called Himself the Son of Man.

4. The Sanhedrin was the high Jewish court. Pilate was the governor. King Herod was visiting Jerusalem for Passover week.

And both things were true.
For indeed He was *both God and Man*.
For Jesus is God.

• • •

It wasn't only that crowd on the hill, or the disciples from a distance who were watching. Satan was watching too, with his warlords and his demons.

All hell was watching.

"What is God *doing*," Satan's warlords said.

"I'm afraid," Satan answered, "He's already done it. He's done just what He said He would do, from the beginning. He's kept that promise He made back in the garden of Eden."

Suddenly the earth began to tremble and shake and the crowds fled in all directions, some in grief, and some in terror, and some in shock.

God's last Passover was finished.

God's Passover Lamb had been slain.

• • •

Later, just before sundown, Nicodemus and Joseph of Arimathea[5] took Jesus down from the cross. They wrapped His body in a linen cloth. They carried Him tenderly, tenderly, to a new tomb in Joseph's garden. And they took Him inside and laid Him down. Then they rolled the huge stone over the entrance.[6]

• • •

"Will He stay there now?" the demons wanted to know.

"He'll go forth in the Spirit to regions in hell," said Satan, "the places He could not go before His crucifixion."

"For what?"

"To herald His accomplished work. To tell them that He actually *did* what He *said* He would do."

---

5. They were members of the Jewish high court; Joseph of Arimathea had gone to Pilate for permission.
6. The "stone" was an enormous disc set in a trough so it could be rolled like a wheel. It took several men to budge it, so they must have had help.

"And then?"

"Then God will raise Him from the dead. We've done everything we could to prevent it, from the beginning of time. But we failed."

"Then all our work has gone down the drain," they glummed.

"Oh no," said Satan, "not at all. Very few will believe it. It's our job to see that they *don't* believe it."

"But we demons believe."

"Yes indeed, there isn't a demon in the Universe or in hell that doesn't believe and tremble," said Satan. "We *know*. We have always known from the beginning."

"But Jesus Himself *told* them God was going to raise Him from the dead," they persisted.

"Of course He did," said Satan, "and they didn't listen. But they'll know soon enough when they see the empty tomb."

"Then they'll believe?"

"No. I *told* you. It's our job to see that they don't."

"How do we manage that?"

"Our job from here on out," said Satan grimly, "is to twist the truth. I'll show you how. I am what Jesus Himself said I am."

"I am a liar."

Checklist

Has God got it all together? Check it out and see:

1. God made a covenant with man.
2. Man blew it.
3. God called out a special NATION for Himself, and chose Abraham to be the father of it, and gave this nation THE PROMISED LAND.
4. God made a covenant with Abraham, gave him a son (Isaac) and promised to bless him if he would obey.
5. God tested Abraham's obedience; Abraham passed the test.
6. God appeared to Isaac's son Jacob and renewed the covenant promise again.
7. God led His NATION (Israel) to Egypt and left them there for 400 years so they could grow in numbers, then raised up Moses to lead them back again to THE PROMISED LAND.

8. God's nation (Israel) got to the very edge of the PROMISED LAND, and blew it again; they had to go back and wander in the wilderness for forty years.

9. Joshua finally led the Israelites over to the PROMISED LAND. They conquered it—*except for a few idols sprinkled here and there.*

10. The "few idols" grew into "many idols" and everyone in the nation "did his own thing." They finally demanded a king.

11. Now the NATION was a KINGDOM! With David (the second king) God renewed the covenant He had made with Adam way back in the garden of Eden, and promised that from *David's family* the Messiah would come—God would come to earth as a man, born as a baby.

12. The great new kingdom prospered, then turned to idol worship and was first divided (Israel and Judah), then conquered, and the Jews went into captivity—some of them disappeared altogether, some of them went to Babylon.

13. In Babylon, God revealed to His prophet Daniel what was to come, right up to the end of times!

But then—four hundred years of silence!

14. Four hundred years later, when the world had grown ENORMOUS and was under Roman rule—God renewed His promise to MARY (who was a descendant of David!). And in David's hometown (Bethlehem) the Messiah was born. And His name was Jesus!

15. John the Baptist told the people that JESUS the MESSIAH was here at last!

16. God had come to earth as a person at last—to keep that promise He'd made to Adam. God loved men so much—*He* was going to pay the ransom and buy man back and deliver him from the slavery of sin, into the freedom of belonging to HIM!

17. In the PROMISED LAND, during the Feast of Passover, JESUS (God's Passover Lamb) was sacrificed (crucified) to buy man back. The ransom was paid. He paid it with His blood! God loves you that much!

CHAPTER 15

"BUT GOD, JESUS HAS GONE BACK TO HEAVEN. IS IT FOR GOOD?"

It was sundown.

The garden of Joseph of Arimathea was quiet, except for the low talking of the soldiers there on watch. They were Temple guards put there by permission of Pilate. For the Jews had gone to him and complained: "We need to put a seal and a guard at the tomb, for if we don't, His disciples may come and carry Him away and try to say that God has raised Him from the dead."

"See to it," Pilate had said, and gave his permission. So the huge circular stone was sealed with Pilate's official seal. And the guards were on watch.

Sounds from the Temple drifted over the air—
"THE LORD REIGNETH . . ."

They were making the evening sacrifice at the Temple.

They were slaying the lamb.

They did not know it, but the Lamb had already been slain that day—"the Lamb of God which taketh away the sins of the world."

• • •

The next day was the Sabbath. There was no business, no haggling over the purchase of groceries, no tourists shopping for souvenirs. The shops were closed.

All the excitement of the day before was gone.

The morning lamb was slain, and then the evening lamb. And the songs were sung each time—
> "IT IS A GOOD THING TO GIVE THANKS
> UNTO THE LORD . . ."

And the Sabbath was over.

"God, You Finally Did It. What Now?"

It was some time during the night when it happened.

An angel of the Lord came down in the twinkling of an eye!

His face shone like lightning and his clothing was a brilliant white.

And he rolled away the stone from the entrance to the tomb as if it were a match box.

AND SAT ON IT!!!

And the soldiers were struck down as if they were dead.

When they came to their senses, they helped each other up and staggered away in terror.

THE TOMB WAS EMPTY.

Quiet, quiet.

Quiet until daybreak.

• • •

Back in Jerusalem, one of the priests climbed to a high place at the top of the Temple and looked toward the east and cried out as he did every morning—

"The morning sun shines!"

And the Temple captain cried back, "Does it light up the sky as far as Hebron?"

"Yea, as far as Hebron!"

And then the age-old ceremony followed.

"Bring in the lamb to be slain!"

"Open the gates of the Temple!"

And the trumpets blew and the lamb was slain and the morning song was sung—
> "THE EARTH IS THE LORD'S" . . .

The sun had risen indeed. Had they but known!

They could have sung
> "The SON is risen! And He lights
> up the whole world!!!!!"[1]

"God, Will They Believe It When They See It?"

"They'll find out soon enough," Satan had said.
And they did!
The women had gone to the tomb.
And found it empty, the stone rolled aside.
Angels told them He had risen.
And He even APPEARED to some of them;
Some of the women,
Especially Mary.
And some of the disciples,
Especially Peter.

And a couple of followers who were not close to Him at all. The Bible doesn't even tell us who they were. And we know only one of their names.

Cleopas.

And it happened this way:

They were trudging along in gloom and disappointment,

When suddenly—

A Stranger was walking alongside them. They hadn't even seen Him coming.

"What are you talking about," the Stranger said, "that has made you so sad."

What? *What*? Could there be somebody around Jerusalem who actually did not know what had been going on?

"Where have you been," they said, "that you don't know what's been going on?"

And they poured the whole story out, weeping as they talked. "We thought that He would redeem Israel, that He would set up His kingdom and save us from the Roman rule. And now He's dead and three days have gone by since these things were done."

---

1. You can read more about this in the book *God and a Boy Named Joe*.

"God, Do You Have to Tell Them *Again*?"

And then the Stranger began to talk. He talked to them about things that had happened from the beginning, when God had first created the world and when Satan had first tempted man and man had fallen and God had promised a Saviour.

And He began to talk to them about Abraham and the *covenant*[2] God had made with him. And how God had told Abraham that from him would come a great and mighty nation.

And then about Isaac,

And Jacob,

And Moses,

And Joshua,

And David.

Especially David. That from David's descendants would come the Messiah.

And how the prophets had told them thousands of years ago that the Messiah would be born in Bethlehem,[3]

And how this Messiah would enter Jerusalem riding upon a donkey,[4]

And how He would be betrayed by one of His own disciples,[5]

And how He would be smitten and abused and spat upon,[6]

And how He would be wounded and bruised for our sins,[7]

And how His hands and feet would be pierced,[8]

And how He would be mocked and insulted,[9]

And how He would be buried in a rich man's tomb,[10]

And how He would rise again,[11]

And how all these things, *all these things*, had happened to Jesus right before their eyes—

2. That contract again with God's promise. Remember?
3. Micah 5:2.
4. Zechariah 9:9.
5. Psalm 41:9.
6. Isaiah 50:6.
7. Isaiah 53:6-12.
8. Zechariah 12:10.
9. Psalm 22:6-8.
10. Isaiah 53:9.
11. Psalm 16:10.

Cleopas and his companion stopped in the middle of the road in absolute astonishment.

"What's It Going to Take to Make Them *Believe* It?"

By this time they were in Emmaus, close to their home.

The Stranger bade them good-bye and started to go on.

"Don't go!"

They cried it out. "Please don't go, come stay with us!"

And the Stranger stayed.

Nothing unusual about that.

They sat down to eat.

Nothing unusual about *that*.

The Stranger said grace. And He took some bread. And broke it. And they gasped in amazement and wonder, sitting there at the table.

The Stranger's hands were pierced!

It was as if God had suddenly opened their eyes and they really *saw* Him for the first time.

It was Jesus Himself!

But at that very moment, He vanished out of their sight.

They never could tell how long they sat there in the late afternoon gloom, in stunned silence.

Then, when the full realization came to them of what had happened, they were galvanized into action.[12] Dinner was forgotten. They no longer had any thought of staying in Emmaus. They had to get back to Jerusalem to tell the others what had happened.

So they made the seven mile trek back, no longer weary. It was as if their feet were shod with seven-league boots. Every step of the way, they talked about it; it seemed they could talk of nothing else.

"Didn't our hearts burn within us," they said, "as He talked with us?" Over it and over it they went until, by the time they got back to where the disciples and other followers of Jesus were, they were on fire!

They could hardly wait to tell it.

But before they could get it out, the disciples burst out with, "The

---

12. They began to make tracks. *Fast.*

Lord has really risen! Some of us actually *saw* Him!"

Wow!

Them too!

Then Cleopas and his companion told their story.

And the disciples told theirs again.

And then they were all talking at once.

And as they talked, suddenly—

Jesus Himself was standing there!

Right *there*, in their midst!

And would you believe it, after all they had seen and heard and felt and talked about, they turned into quivering cowards and trembled like Jello in a high wind. They thought they were seeing a ghost!

"Why are you frightened?" Jesus said. "Do you *still* doubt? Look at Me. Look at My hands. Look at My feet. *Touch* Me."

And He held out His hands for them to see the marks from the nails, and He showed them the wounds in His feet.

And then He did a very practical thing. He asked them if they had anything to eat.

They gave Him a piece of broiled fish, and as they stood there dumbfounded, He ate it.

"God, How Patient Can You Get?"

"Don't you remember," He said after He had finished eating, "Don't you remember I told you that everything written about Me would all come true? Don't you remember all the covenants[13] God made with Abraham and Jacob and Moses and David? And the promise He made to David that the Messiah would come from David's family? Don't you remember that the Messiah must suffer and die and rise again from the dead on the third day?"

And He began to explain to them again,

Gently,

Patiently,

All that He had told them and told them and told them, *He told them again*.

What a Bible class it was!

13. You're right, contracts.

Never was there a Bible class like it, when the students listened in such rapt attention and joy. They hung on His every word. They listened, hardly daring to breathe lest they miss something.

When He finished, He said, "Now you have seen most of these things come true."

"*Most* of These Things? You Mean There's More?"

"There's more?" they said in wonder.

"There's more," He said.

And there *was* more.

He kept appearing to them again and again, and always when they least expected it. What wonderful days they were!

Ten days, twenty days,

They couldn't get enough of what He had to say.

Thirty days, forty days—

And then suddenly it was all over.

"I am going to My Father," He told them. "But I will return."

"When?" they begged, "*When?*"

"The Father sets those dates—they are not for you to know," He said. "But when the Holy Spirit has come upon you, you will receive power."

Power?!?

"Yes, power to preach about My death and resurrection, throughout the earth."

• • •

It was not long after that, when He led them out along the road to Bethany.

And when they got to the Mount of Olives, He stopped,

And lifted His hands to heaven,

And He blessed them.

And then He rose into the sky before their very eyes,

And disappeared into a cloud, leaving them standing there staring. They never knew how long they stood there, straining their eyes toward the sky.

But suddenly two men, *two white-robed men*, were standing there alongside them.

Angels!

"Why are you standing there staring at the sky?" they said.

"Jesus has gone away to heaven."

But that was not all. "And some day," the men said, "just as He went, He will return."

The disciples turned around and started back down the hill to Jerusalem, like men in a dream. They could scarcely speak, so filled were they with the things that they had heard and seen.

They were to stay in Jerusalem and wait, they remembered that.

Stay in Jerusalem.

There was more to come.

They did not know exactly what it would be or how it would happen, but there was more to come.

Jesus had told them to *wait until the Holy Spirit had come upon them*.

The Holy Spirit?

What did that mean?

"God—*No*. Don't Let Satan Spoil It Now!"

"What now?" said Satan's warlords.

"Send some demons to them at once," Satan said, "Inject into their minds the spirit of doubt and the spirit of impatience."

"Yes sire," they said, "Anything else?"

"That will do for the moment."

They turned to leave.

"And see that they don't pray!" he called out after them. "Above all, don't let them gather together to pray!"

"Right!" they called back.

And they scrambled off.

"That," Satan muttered as they left, "would be our undoing for sure."

Checklist

Has God got it all together? Check it out and see:

1. God made a covenant with man.

2. Man blew it.

3. God called out a special NATION for Himself, and chose Abraham to be the father of it, and gave this nation THE PROMISED LAND.

4. God made a covenant with Abraham, gave him a son (Isaac) and promised to bless him if he would obey.

5. God tested Abraham's obedience; Abraham passed the test.

6. God appeared to Isaac's son Jacob and renewed the covenant promise again.

7. God led His NATION (Israel) to Egypt and left them there for 400 years so they could grow in numbers, then raised up Moses to lead them back again to THE PROMISED LAND.

8. God's nation (Israel) got to the very edge of the PROMISED LAND, and blew it again; they had to go back and wander in the wilderness for forty years.

9. Joshua finally led the Israelites over to the PROMISED LAND. They conquered it—*except for a few idols sprinkled here and there*.

10. The "few idols" grew into "many idols" and everyone in the nation "did his own thing." They finally demanded a king.

11. Now the NATION was a KINGDOM! With David (the second king) God renewed the covenant He had made with Adam way back in the garden of Eden, and promised that from *David's family* the Messiah would come—God would come to earth as a man, born as a baby.

12. The great new kingdom prospered, then turned to idol worship and was first divided (Israel and Judah), then conquered, and the Jews went into captivity—some of them disappeared altogether, some of them went to Babylon.

13. In Babylon, God revealed to His prophet Daniel what was to come, right up to the end of times!

But then—four hundred years of silence!

14. Four hundred years later, when the world had grown ENORMOUS and was under Roman rule—God renewed His promise to MARY (who was a descendant of David!). And in David's hometown (Bethlehem) the Messiah was born. And His name was Jesus!

15. John the Baptist told the people that JESUS the MESSIAH was here at last!

16. God had come to earth as a person at last—to keep that promise He'd made to Adam. God loved men so much—*He* was going to pay the ransom and buy man back and deliver him from the slavery of sin, into the freedom of belonging to HIM!

17. In the PROMISED LAND, during the Feast of Passover, JESUS (God's Passover Lamb) was sacrificed (crucified) to buy man back. The ransom was paid. He paid it with His blood! God loves you that much!

18. Jesus rose from the dead and went back to heaven. The sacrifice was accepted, the deal was closed!

CHAPTER 16

"GOD, YOU MEAN YOU ACTUALLY PUT ALL THIS IN WRITING?"

"Jesus Is Gone—*Now* What?"

"Don't let them pray." Satan had told his warlords.

But in spite of all the warlords and demons could do, Jesus' followers spent their time either in the Temple blessing God, or in an upper room—

Doing *what*?

Praying.

Ten more days went by. And then the day of the Feast of Pentecost[1] came.

It was like the week of the Passover all over again, or nearly so. The city was jammed with worshipers from nations all over the country. There were the services and the Temple, and the sacrifices, and the jostling and the gossiping.

But the disciples and about a hundred followers of Jesus were gathered together in that upper room somewhere in Jerusalem.

It was nine o'clock in the morning.

"Now Your Holy Spirit? Wow!"

Suddenly, a sound like the roaring of a mighty wind rushed into the skies above them and filled the house where they were.

And then what looked like tongues of fire filled the room,

And settled on their heads.

And then,

They began to speak in other languages.

The Holy Spirit had come!

And the crowds from all over Jerusalem came arunning, to the place where the disciples were,

---

1. The Feast of Pentecost was also called the "Feast of Weeks," or "Week of Weeks," because it was seven weeks after the Passover.

And heard the disciples speak,
But not in their native tongue.
They were speaking in *other* tongues and *other* languages.

And every man listening, no matter what language he spoke, understood exactly what they were saying, each man in his own language.

It sounded like a murmur at first, then the crowds were shouting.
"They're drunk!"
"THEY'RE DRUNK!"
And then one of the apostles[2] stepped forward.

"We are not drunk," he shouted. "But you have seen what was predicted by one of our own prophets—the prophet Joel—who predicted that God would pour out His Holy Spirit on believers!"

Now the crowd was quiet.

And the apostle—who was *Peter*—went on to explain all of God's contracts, from Abraham on down to that very day.

Peter, at long last, had it all together!
From Abraham, a nation.
Then from David, a family.
And then finally, from David's descendant, Mary—
The Messiah.

And this Messiah was the same Jesus Christ whom they had crucified.

It was absolutely earth shattering.

And three thousand of those people in that crowd believed and accepted Jesus as the Son of God, and were baptized.

The new church was born!

"God, It's Getting Better and *Better*."

Satan and his warlords had a strategy meeting.

"They reached 3,000 people for Jesus," the warlords glummed, "in one morning."

---

2. The disciples were going to be called "apostles" from then on. An apostle is "one who is sent forth."

"I know, I know," said Satan, "Something has to be done to stop them. Get them arrested. Get them flogged. Molest them, bug them, maybe they'll get discouraged."

"It doesn't look good," they said, "no matter what we do."

"It's going to get worse," said Satan. "Filled with the power of the Holy Spirit of God, these men are going to start turning the world upside down. They'll even start performing miracles."

• • •

And they did.

The first thing Peter and John did was heal a hopelessly crippled beggar in Jesus' name.

And every time any of the apostles performed a miracle, they preached a sermon. They talked about all the covenants[3] that God had made, and what the covenants had meant.

They told what the prophets had said, how it all fit together.

"God has got it all together," they said, "if you'll only listen!"

And what happened?

They were in and out of prison faster than you can read it. They were threatened. They were beaten. But nothing could stop them, nothing.

"Nor can we stop them from praying," complained the demons. "They pray in spite of anything we can do. And every time they get up from their knees they get up with another bucketful of courage and power."

It was true.

Every day was a miracle day.

People were healed. The sick and the lame and the blind and the deaf.

And as fast as the apostles were put in prison, God sent His angels in the night to let them out again.

Even death didn't stop them.

Yes, one of their leaders was grabbed by the religious leaders and stoned to death. A young man by the name of Stephen. This might have stopped the rest of them cold, except for one thing. Just before

3. The contracts, the contracts with God's Promises. Got it?

Stephen died, he cried out "I see the heavens opened! And I see JESUS STANDING at the right hand of God!"

If any one of them was discouraged, that took care of it.

"Did you hear what Stephen said before he died?" Satan's warlords fumed. "He saw Jesus STANDING at the right hand of God. Nothing will be able to stop them now."

"Satan Hasn't Given Up Yet?"

Satan thought about that for a moment.

"All isn't lost," he said at last. "I still have a few tricks up my sleeve."

"You've thought of something?" they said.

"Oh yes," said Satan. "It just takes a little time. The thing to do is to scatter them. If they're scattered they won't be as powerful. And I've got just the person to do it."

"Who?"

"Saul of Tarsus," he said. "He's a Pharisee. One of the religious leaders."

"But the Pharisees haven't had much clout so far," they said.

"Ah," said Satan, "this one will. He is one of the best educated[4] and most influential Pharisees of our day. And he hates this new church. He has plans to *pulverize* it."

"Ah," they said, "a man to admire."

"He'll play right into my hands," said Satan. "He's already going about like an angry bull, arresting believers and dragging them out of their homes and hauling them up to the Sanhedrin. What's more, he has plans to branch out. He already has permission from the high priest to go abroad and drag Christians out of their homes and haul them back here to the Sanhedrin. His plans now are to go to Damascus."

"To *Damascus*?"

"Yes. If anyone can keep this church from spreading, Saul can do so. Very influential man, *very* influential."

"Oh," they said, brightening considerably. "Our cause is in good hands."

---

4. The famous Gamaliel was Saul's teacher; he would have been in "Who's Who" today.

"Good hands indeed," said Satan. "And now, before we conclude this meeting, a word of caution. I can't be in every place at once, so you must be alert. No slumbering, no goofing off. Prowl around like hungry roaring lions, looking for victims to tear apart.[5] I'll be wandering to and fro, but we can always keep in touch. As you know, the earth is getting bigger all the time. And I have other countries to go to, although I must say most of them are pretty well under my control."

"Yes sire," they said.

"Report to me again in due time. Our next meeting should be a good one."

"Right on, sire."

"Does Your Holy Spirit Affect *Everybody* Like This?"

But their next meeting was a fiasco.[6]

"Well, we'll take some of the lesser lights first," said Satan. "What of their other deacons? What of Philip? I trust you've kept him under control."

"Sire," they said, "Philip is completely *out* of control. When the church began to scatter, he went to Samaria. He's been preaching there. And he's sensational. The throngs come to hear him. And the sick and the lame and the blind are healed and God is adding believers to the church by the thousands. And the rest of the apostles are bad news too."

"Rats," said Satan. "All right, all right, we'll just go down the list and check them all out."

And they did.

It was bad news all the way.

"Well, at least we've got Saul under our thumb. I'm counting heavily on him," said Satan. "What of him?"

"That's the really bad news," they said. "He was on his way to Damascus, when suddenly a great light from heaven blazed down upon him. And he fell down in terror into the dust. And a voice said to him, 'Saul, why are you persecuting Me?' And Saul asked who it was."

5. See I Peter 5:8.
6. A mess.

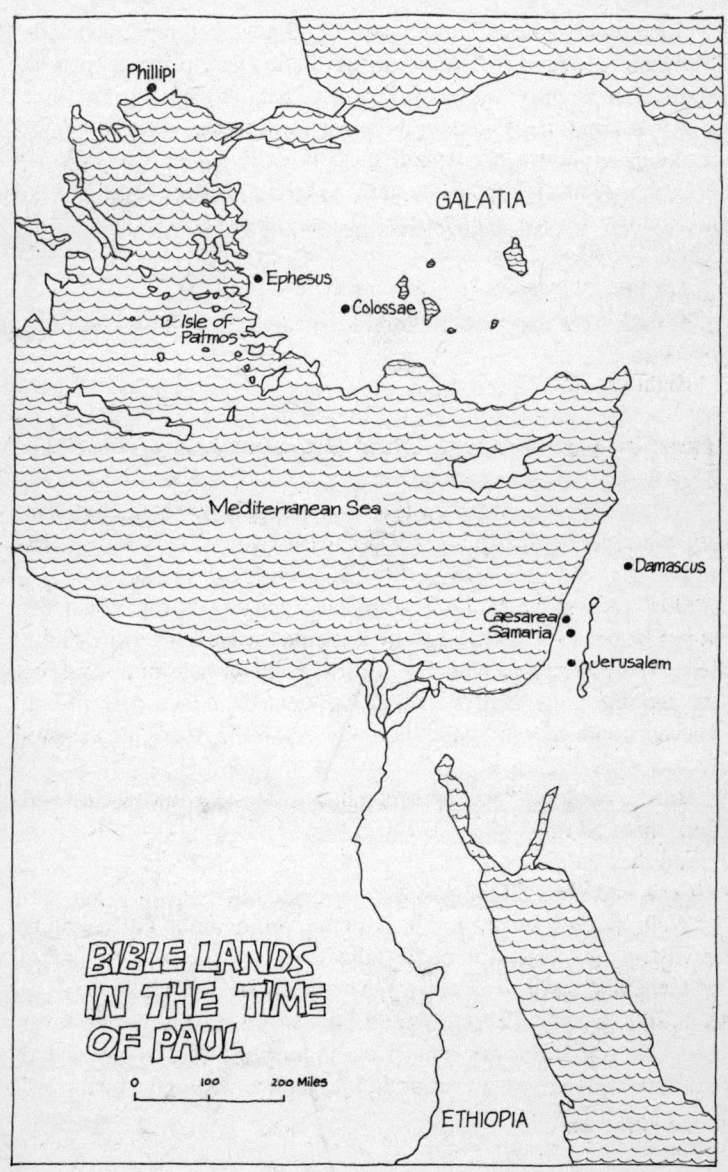

"And?" said Satan.

"Well it was Jesus Himself. And the power of the Holy Spirit filled Saul and now all he can cry out is 'Jesus is indeed the Son of God.'"

Satan let out a cry of such hatred it was terrible to hear.

"Make his road rough!" he shrieked. And then, "Is there more?"

"Yes," they said, "Peter went to Caesarea to visit a Roman army officer who called for him. The officer and all of his family and their servants turned their lives over to God. So now this gospel has gone to the Gentiles."

Satan put his head in his hands and rocked himself back and forth and moaned.

"Oh yes," they added, "and we forgot to tell you. Philip, during his travels, ran into an Ethiopian and told *him* about God. He is the Treasurer of Queen Candace of Ethiopia. He's gone home and told it. And now it's all over Ethiopia too."

"It will be all over the world if we can't stop it," Satan grumbled.

"They can't be tempted," they said. "As fast as we get them thrown into prison, God sends His angels and gets them out again. We get them beaten and they come through praising the Lord."

"Enough, enough," cried Satan. "It's got to stop somewhere. It can't get any worse."

"But it *is* getting worse," they said.

"I know human nature," Satan insisted. "Sooner or later it's bound to peter out. Those people are going to forget what they've been told. And those new churches that are being established—they'll run out of gas. Just give them time."

"God, Isn't There Anything You Haven't Thought Of?"

But as the reports from his warlords and demons came pouring in, his hopes were dashed. For it was soon apparent that these new Christians would not be allowed to forget what they'd been told. It was all being put down in writing!

"In writing!" Satan bellowed. "What do you mean?"

"The apostles are not only establishing churches, they are writing letters of instruction to them, for the people to read to each other and study."

"Well, it shouldn't be too difficult to mix them up," said Satan. "Make them think they've got to earn God's forgiveness by sacrificing lambs. Make them think the whole business is for the Jews alone."

"But what of the letter that Saul, whose Roman name is Paul—"

"I know, I know," said Satan. "What about him?"

"Well what about the letter he wrote to the Romans? In that letter he says, 'For I am not ashamed of this Good News about Christ. It is God's powerful method of bringing *all* who believe it to heaven. This message was preached *first* to the Jews alone, but *now everyone is invited to come to God in this same way* . . . This is accomplished from start to finish by *faith* . . . the man who finds life will find it through trusting God.' "[7]

"All right. Make them think that's not enough," Satan said.

"Ah, but again," they said, "in Paul's letter he says 'So now, since we have been made right in God's sight by faith in his promises, we can have real peace with him because of what Jesus Christ our Lord has done for us.' "[8]

"All right, all *right*. Don't let them learn any more than that. Keep them like babies. Let them drink only milk."

"Ah, but sire," they said, "Paul has written a letter to the church in Ephesus and told them that they had to grow up . . . until they all become full grown in the Lord . . ."[9]

"We can sneak around it, we can sneak around it," Satan said. "They don't even have to know we're here."

"Ah," they said, "but Paul has already written them that we are here. He has told them that they are fighting against the evil rulers of the unseen world—"

"That's us," said Satan.

"—Mighty Satanic beings, THE GREAT EVIL PRINCES OF DARKNESS WHO RULE THIS WORLD. And against huge numbers of wicked spirits in the spirit world. He has told them to put on the armor of God—to resist us when we attack, to put on the belt of truth and the breastplate of God's approval—"

---

7. Romans 1:16,17.
8. Romans 5:1.
9. See Ephesians 4:13.

"He told them that?"

"—And the shield of faith to stop the fiery darts aimed at them by us. And the sword of the Spirit which is the Word of God. All this so they'll be able to stand safe against our tricks—"[10]

"Enough!" cried Satan, "I've heard enough! I don't care how much they know in their heads. Just so long as they don't *practice* it."

"Ah," they said, "but they are taught to practice it. The apostle James wrote and told them that they should give of their money and give of their time and take care of the poor and—"

"This I do not like," said Satan, "Oh this I do not like one little bit. Now they're messing around."

"—And also that their faith will be dead if it's not the kind that results in good deeds,"[11] they added lamely.

"Worse than I thought," said Satan, "Much worse than I thought. There's only one thing left, and that is to get them to fight."

"Ah, but the apostle John wrote them to love one another."

"What do they know about love?" said Satan, "What do they know about love?"

"Why John wrote them," they said, "'We know what real love is, from Christ's example in dying for us. And so we also ought to lay down our lives for our Christian brothers.'[12] And there's more."

"I don't think I can stand any more," Satan said wearily.

"But the *other* apostles wrote letters."

"I don't want to hear them. Dull the peoples' minds. Brainwash them. Make them blind."

"But we can't confuse all of them."

"We must do the best we can," said Satan. "We must confuse them about what's already happened. And we must keep them, if possible, from knowing what's *going* to happen. Especially that Jesus is going to come back again."

"But Jesus already told them He was coming back again," they said.

"What of it?" he said. "He told them He was going to rise again and

10. Read Ephesians 6:11-18.
11. See James 2:26.
12. I John 3:16.

they didn't believe that, did they? Why should they believe He's coming again?"

"God, Satan Is Running *Scared*."

"What about Nebuchadnezzar's dream? And what Daniel told him? The kingdom of gold—the kingdom of silver—the kingdom of—"

"I know, I know. You don't have to give me a history lesson," he grumbled.

"But Daniel also told them about the stone—"

"Bite your tongue!" howled Satan. "Don't even mention it. Besides, in their minds, that dream is a thing of the past. It happened so long ago. Give them enough time and they'll forget Nebuchadnezzar ever *had* a dream. Or that there ever *was* a Daniel. I'm far more worried about the apostles than I am about Daniel."

"Well at least we don't have John to worry about," they said. "He's been exiled."

"Exiled? Where?"

"To the Isle of Patmos. It's way out in the boondocks."

"No matter, no matter," said Satan. "Dispatch some of your demons there anyhow. And supply them with some fiery darts in case they're needed."

"They won't be needed. Not in that God-forsaken place," they said.

Satan bristled. "There is no God-forsaken place. Just remember that. Don't underestimate God. He's everywhere."

His warlords and demons dashed off to do his bidding.

"Still," he mused to himself as they left, "I don't see what possible harm John can do us on Patmos. . . ."

Checklist

Has God got it all together? Check it out and see:

1. God made a covenant with man.
2. Man blew it.
3. God called out a special NATION for Himself, and chose Abraham to be the father of it, and gave this nation THE PROMISED LAND.

4. God made a covenant with Abraham, gave him a son (Isaac) and promised to bless him if he would obey.

5. God tested Abraham's obedience; Abraham passed the test.

6. God appeared to Isaac's son Jacob and renewed the covenant promise again.

7. God led His NATION (Israel) to Egypt and left them there for 400 years so they could grow in numbers, then raised up Moses to lead them back again to THE PROMISED LAND.

8. God's nation (Israel) got to the very edge of the PROMISED LAND, and blew it again; they had to go back and wander in the wilderness for forty years.

9. Joshua finally led the Israelites over to the PROMISED LAND. They conquered it—*except for a few idols sprinkled here and there*.

10. The "few idols" grew into "many idols" and everyone in the nation "did his own thing." They finally demanded a king.

11. Now the NATION was a KINGDOM! With David (the second king) God renewed the covenant He had made with Adam way back in the garden of Eden, and promised that from *David's family* the Messiah would come—God would come to earth as a man, born as a baby.

12. The great new kingdom prospered, then turned to idol worship and was first divided (Israel and Judah), then conquered, and the Jews went into captivity—some of them disappeared altogether, some of them went to Babylon.

13. In Babylon, God revealed to His prophet Daniel what was to come, right up to the end of times!

But then—four hundred years of silence!

14. Four hundred years later, when the world had grown ENORMOUS and was under Roman rule—God renewed His promise to MARY (who was a descendant of David!) And in David's hometown (Bethlehem) the Messiah was born. And His name was Jesus!

15. John the Baptist told the people that JESUS the MESSIAH was here at last!

16. God had come to earth as a person at last—to keep that promise He'd made to Adam. God loved men so much—*He* was going to pay

the ransom and buy man back and deliver him from the slavery of sin, into the freedom of belonging to HIM!

17. In the PROMISED LAND, during the Feast of Passover, JESUS (God's Passover Lamb) was sacrificed (crucified) to buy man back. The ransom was paid. He paid it with His blood! God loves you that much.

18. Jesus rose from the dead and went back to heaven. The sacrifice was accepted, the deal was closed!

19. The Holy Spirit of God came down from heaven and descended upon the disciples (now called apostles) and gave them GREAT POWER AND UNDERSTANDING they had never had before. They scattered in all directions to tell people about Jesus, and some of them wrote letters to the new believers to instruct them and encourage them. These letters, along with the Old Testament Scriptures, were all inspired by the Holy Spirit and are OUR BIBLE.

CHAPTER 17

"GOD, YOU MEAN YOU REALLY HAVE IT ALL TOGETHER? AND JESUS IS COMING AGAIN?"

Patmos.

A tiny wind-swept island in the Aegean Sea. It rose out of the sea, bleak and threatening, its coastline ragged, its surface rocky and treeless. Surely not a place to live. The only people there were political prisoners exiled there by the Roman government. And of course Roman soldiers. And guards. And a few minor government officials.

And the apostle John.[1]

But John didn't look at the prison-like bleakness. He looked above and beyond it. As far as he could see in every direction were peaks of other islands, and the great expanse of the Aegean Sea. And way off on the horizon, the distant volcano of Santorin, like the backdrop in an operetta.

And though he didn't know it, he was there on Patmos because he had a rendezvous[2] with the One Person who was the beginning and the end, the A and Z of the great plan of God.

"Is This What Jesus Is Really Like?"

It was the Lord's day.

John was worshiping.

When suddenly,

He heard a loud voice behind him. It sounded like a trumpet blast. "I am the A and Z, the first and the last!" the voice cried. And then, "Write down everything you see."

1. John was there for telling what he knew about Jesus.
2. Ron-day-voo. It's a meeting by appointment.

And John turned to see who was speaking.

There, standing, was One who looked like Jesus, wearing a long white robe, circled with a golden band across his chest. His hair was white as wool or snow, and his eyes were like flames of fire. His feet gleamed like burnished bronze, and his voice thundered like the waves against the shore.[3]

John fell at His feet like a dead man.

Why Daniel had seen that same One, standing beside the great Tigris River.

Yes!

Daniel had looked up, and there standing before him was Jesus robed in linen garments, with a belt of purest gold around His waist. From His face had come blinding flashes like lightning, His arms and feet had shone like polished brass, and His voice had been like the roaring of a vast multitude of people.[4]

And now He was standing before John.

It was none other than Jesus Himself.

Astonishing!

"Why Jesus Has *Always* Been Around!"

"Don't be afraid," Jesus said, "Though I am the First and the Last, the Living One who died and is now alive forevermore, Who has the keys of hell and death—don't be afraid! Write down what you have just seen and what will soon be shown to you."

In all his life, John had never imagined that he would see anything like this.

Jesus had appeared to Abraham in the form of a man, in front of Abraham's tent, to tell him that his son Isaac would be born.

He had appeared to Jacob as a man, in the dead of the night, and wrestled with him and changed his name to Israel.

He had appeared to Moses up on top of the mountain when Moses had gone up to get the Ten Commandments.

And He had appeared to many of the prophets, down through the ages.

3. Read Revelation 1:14,15.
4. Read Daniel 10:4-6.

But this!

Except for Daniel, there had been nothing like this!

"You Mean There's Really More to Come?"

John had one of the greatest privileges ever known to man. To write down, not only what *had* happened, or what was happening—but what was *going* to happen!

Slowly, slowly, in vision after vision, Jesus showed John what was yet to come.

And slowly, slowly John wrote it all down.[5]

The days went by, and the weeks and the months.

And what was revealed to John on the Isle of Patmos was so wonderful, so marvelous, that there was only one word for it.

Indescribable.

How could he ever write it down? Who would ever understand it? Why no mere man has ever seen or even imagined what wonderful things God has ready for those who love Him.[6]

But, as best he could, and in the only language he had, he wrote down what the visions told him.

"You Really Are for Real."

And as he wrote, he remembered—Jesus Himself had already told them a great deal. They just hadn't been *listening*.

Slowly the pieces fell together.

And the picture began to emerge.

"God, Is Satan Really 'Licked'?"

"I've gathered you together," said Satan, "from all four corners of the earth, because I want a full report on what's happening. Everywhere."

"The news is bad," they said.

"Bad where?" said Satan.

---

5. John was on Patmos about a year and a half. We don't know how long it took him to write it down. He may have written some of it when he went back to Ephesus to live.
6. I Corinthians 2:9.

"Bad everywhere," they said.

"Even on Patmos?"

"Even on Patmos. Jesus Himself is revealing Himself to John there. As a matter of fact, that is why John was exiled to Patmos. He didn't know it but he had an appointment with Jesus."

"And?"

"And Jesus is right now revealing to John everything that's going to happen."

"How?"

"In visions that are hard to understand. Even John can hardly find the words to write them down."

"Well then," said Satan, "We have nothing to worry about. He did that to Daniel thousands of years ago. And other prophets too. Jeremiah. Ezekiel. Isaiah. Zechariah. All of them. And how many have believed or understood what they wrote? Very few. So you see—"

"God, I Never Knew Your Word Was So Important."

"We would have nothing to worry about," they said, "if it were only Patmos. But at various times Jesus has appeared to the other apostles and they are writing letters to the churches, telling *them* what's going to happen. Especially Paul."

"Oh," moaned Satan, "Paul has been a thorn in my side ever since he saw Jesus on the way to Damascus."

"Well, he's been writing letters to the churches for some time. But the letters he just wrote to the churches in Thessalonica and Corinth can do us the most damage yet. He tells them quite explicitly[7] what's going to happen."

Satan glowered and waited.

"It's that all the bits and pieces are coming together," they went on, "This is our problem. If they don't understand *one* part they will understand *another*. And bit by bit and piece by piece they'll put them all together and they will finally understand it *all*. These letters can do us a lot of damage."

"Bah," said Satan, "and humbug. These letters are just being passed

7. Loud and clear.

around to little churches here and there. They can't possibly do any harm. Just keep them from leaking out, if you can. In a few years they'll be forgotten."

"But what if," they said, "what *if*—some day, somehow, they get it into their heads to put all these letters together and publish them? Then they'll have every bit and every piece. If this ever happens, we are undone."

"It will happen," said Satan, "We can only hope to scramble their thinking so they won't understand it. We can make it look like foolishness to them. Get them so preoccupied with the delights and problems of this world that they can't see beyond their noses."

"We'll do our best," they said, "to befuddle them."

"It's going to be a battle to the finish," he said.

There was a long silence. They knew that in the end they would lose.

"But in the meantime," said Satan, "we can cause a great deal of trouble, a *great* deal of trouble. Just remember I'm the biggest liar in the Universe. Meanwhile, get busy."

• • •

Satan's worst fears came true, of course.

Down through the ages, men did get it all put together—from the first records that Moses wrote, to the revelation that Jesus gave John on Patmos.

Every bit and every piece came together. It's the Bible.

And it tells us about the end times, and the coming of Jesus.

"I Have More Questions: WHEN Is He Coming?"

The Bible doesn't tell us exactly when. Jesus said, "No one knows the date and the hour when the end will be—not even the angels. There will be no warning. People will be going about their daily business, eating and drinking, buying and selling and farming and building. It will be 'business as usual,' right up to the hour of My return."[8]

8. See Matthew 24:36-38.

So the answer is: "Could be any minute!"

"Then How Will I Know? I Might Miss Him!"

You'll know, all right. There'll be no secret about it. *Everybody* will know.[9] "The Lord himself will come down from heaven with a mighty shout and with the soul-stirring cry of the archangel and the great trumpet-call of God."

"And Then What?!?"

Well, then, two things will happen—one right after the other. And it will all happen in a moment, in the twinkling of an eye! First, all believers who have died, will suddenly become alive with *new bodies*, and will be caught up to meet Jesus *in the air*. And right after that, all believers who are still alive will suddenly have *their* new bodies and be caught up in the air too![10]

"New Bodies? What Will They Be Like?"

Remember what Jesus' body was like after He was raised from the dead? He could eat, He could talk, He could pass through walls and locked doors, He could suddenly appear, and just as suddenly disappear? Well, our new bodies will be just like that. And they will never get sick, and they will never grow old. But even though our bodies will be brand new—we will all know each other.[11]

"What Then, What Then?"

Those who are left upon the earth will have a time of trouble—a period known in the Bible as the Tribulation. The whole world will be ruled by a dictator. In the Bible, he is called the Antichrist. This is where Satan comes back into the picture.

"Yessss," hissed Satan to his warlords. "I will enter into the Antichrist and tell my lies through him. He will promise the world peace[12] and the people will follow him. He will set himself up as God

---

9. I Thessalonians 4:16.
10. Read I Thessalonians 4:16,17 and I Corinthians 15:50-53.
11. Read the Scripture again.
12. Daniel 11:12.

and demand worship from all the world. And at last, through the Antichrist I will have what I've always wanted from the beginning—to be worshiped as God."

"And the people will rebel against God," his warlords prompted.

"Yes," said Satan, gloating.

"Where?" they wanted to know.

"Why in a place called Armageddon—a place in northern Israel—the Promised Land. Where else? It'll be the largest army ever to assemble in the history of the world."

"Then," his warlords said, "Jesus will come from heaven with His heavenly army and—"

"I'd rather not discuss that part of it," said Satan.

"But He told John at Patmos He will defeat us all with a word—with just a word from His mouth," they insisted. "And we'll be captured and thrown into the lake of fire—"

"I don't want to discuss it!" Satan shrieked.

"Phew! What Happens Then? Is Everybody Destroyed?"

No, not at all. During this time of trouble, great numbers of people will have come to believe on Jesus. And among them, vast numbers of Jews will have been converted. Jesus will come to earth again—to set up His Kingdom for a thousand years—this time bringing with Him all of those who had been caught up in the air with Him when He came before.

"You're a Part of God's Plan, Too."

Yes, you too. You will come back with Him, and rule with Him, and He will sit—of all places—upon the throne of David. And the promise that God made to Israel will come true at last. Jesus will reign. And you will reign with Him. A reign of peace and prosperity!

"What Comes After the Thousand Years?"

Satan will be loosed for a little while.

"When I'm loosed again," he said, "I'll—"

"But," his warlords said, "it'll only be for a little while."

"Never you mind," said Satan, "In that little while I'll cause as much trouble as I can. I'll stir up all those who still do not believe in God, who still rebel against Him. And I'll gather them together for battle—and go the length and breadth of the earth, surrounding the believers and—"

He didn't finish. They all sat in a gloomy silence. They knew that the fire of God would come down from heaven and devour them. And that they would be cast into the lake of fire for ever and ever.

And never be loosed again.

"But What's This I Hear About a Last Judgment? Will I Be Judged?"

No. The last judgment before the great white throne of God will be for the people who had absolutely refused to believe in God, and whose names were never written in the Book of Life.

There's *another* judgment—the JUDGMENT SEAT OF CHRIST.[13] And there, *believers* will be judged according to *what they've done for Jesus*, to see how they stack up as Christians, and to get their rewards.

"Home at Last!"

And then—

Heaven!

There was no way that John could describe it. It was beautiful beyond description. He had to use the only words he knew. It is made of gold.

It is clear as glass.

It's adorned with precious stones.

It's lighted by God's glory.

We'll be able to understand all things.

There'll be no sin, no death, no pain. God will wipe away all tears.

All this—and our new glorious bodies too!

"Check Yourself Out. Will You Be There?"

Jesus wants you to be there. God planned from the very beginning

---

13. For believers only!

of the world that you should be there.

The whole Bible is one story, one plan, God's plan for YOU, so you CAN be there!

And in His revelation to John on Patmos, He said, "Behold, I stand at the door and knock."[14]

He's saying, "Listen. I'm standing here knocking at the door of your life. And if you'll open it and invite Me into your life, I'll come in and live *with* you and *through* you."

Let Him in right now, if you never have before. And *your* name will be written in the Book of Life.

You have nothing to fear.

God is right on schedule.

He's never early.

And He's never late.

He's right on time.

Some of the last words God has for us in the Bible are:

"I am Jesus. I am coming soon.[15] And My reward is with Me."

And our response should be one of welcome.

"Amen! Come quickly, Lord Jesus!"[16]

Checklist

Has God got it all together? Check it out and see:

1. God made a covenant with man.

2. Man blew it.

3. God called out a special NATION for Himself, and chose Abraham to be the father of it, and gave this nation THE PROMISED LAND.

4. God made a covenant with Abraham, gave him a son (Isaac) and promised to bless him if he would obey.

5. God tested Abraham's obedience; Abraham passed the test.

6. God appeared to Isaac's son Jacob and renewed the covenant promise again.

7. God led His NATION (Israel) to Egypt and left them there for

---

14. Read Revelation 3:20,21.
15. Unexpectedly.
16. Read Revelation 22:12-21.

400 years so they could grow in numbers, then raised up Moses to lead them back again to THE PROMISED LAND.

8. God's nation (Israel) got to the very edge of the PROMISED LAND, and blew it again; they had to go back and wander in the wilderness for forty years.

9. Joshua finally led the Israelites over to the PROMISED LAND. They conquered it—*except for a few idols sprinkled here and there*.

10. The "few idols" grew into "many idols" and everyone in the nation "did his own thing." They finally demanded a king.

11. Now the NATION was a KINGDOM! With David (the second king) God renewed the covenant He had made with Adam way back in the garden of Eden, and promised that from *David's family* the Messiah would come—God would come to earth as a man, born as a baby.

12. The great new kingdom prospered, then turned to idol worship and was first divided (Israel and Judah), then conquered, and the Jews went into captivity—some of them disappeared altogether, some of them went to Babylon.

13. In Babylon, God revealed to His prophet Daniel what was to come, right up to the end of times!

But then—four hundred years of silence!

14. Four hundred years later, when the world had grown ENORMOUS and was under Roman rule—God renewed His promise to MARY (who was a descendant of David!) And in David's hometown (Bethlehem) the Messiah was born. And His name was Jesus.

15. John the Baptist told the people that JESUS the MESSIAH was here at last!

16. God had come to earth as a person at last—to keep that promise He'd made to Adam. God loved men so much—*He* was going to pay the ransom and buy man back and deliver him from the slavery of sin, into the freedom of belonging to HIM!

17. In the PROMISED LAND, during the Feast of Passover, JESUS (God's Passover Lamb) was sacrificed (crucified) to buy man back. The ransom was paid. He paid it with His blood! God loves you that much.

18. Jesus rose from the dead and went back to heaven. The sacrifice was accepted, the deal was closed!

19. The Holy Spirit of God came down from heaven and descended upon the disciples (now called apostles) and gave them GREAT POWER AND UNDERSTANDING they had never had before. They scattered in all directions to tell people about Jesus, and some of them wrote letters to the new believers to instruct them and encourage them. These letters, along with the Old Testament Scriptures, were all inspired by the Holy Spirit and are OUR BIBLE.

20. Jesus is coming again! He has said so, and it will come true, just as everything else He has ever said, since creation, has come true. YES, GOD'S GOT IT ALL TOGETHER!!

EPILOGUE

"NO MORE QUESTIONS, GOD."

Dear God:
  Wow!
  It really *is* all one story. And it sure is taking You long enough to tell it. I guess it seems long to us because You don't live in time and we do. But the idea that I figure in *all* of it, and that You had *me* in mind when You first began it, is the most exciting piece of news I've ever had!
  And the idea that You're standing there knocking at the door of my heart and my personality, waiting for me to ask You in, is almost more than I can handle. I'll come right out and say it: I'm going to invite Jesus into my life now, to stay with me and be my friend—for life, and for evermore.
  Wow!
  I'm with You! For You really do have it all together—and always have . . .

                    Signed